DISASTER!

1. Press photographers in the rain. Lockerbie,
January 4 1989.

Over the last 100 years Scotland has seen
some of Britain's worst disasters

Britain's worst aviation disaster at Lockerbie in 1988
Britain's worst rail crash at Gretna in 1915
The world's worst oilrig disaster in the North Sea
off Aberdeen in 1988
Britain's worst peacetime naval disaster at Stornoway in 1919
The worst disaster in the British cinema industry at Paisley
in 1929
The world's worst civil helicopter disaster off Shetland
in 1986

The story in words and pictures of these
and more than 100 other disasters

2. The human face of disaster in the streets of Lockerbie
on the day of the Memorial Service, January 4 1989.

DISASTER!

One Hundred Years of
Wreck, Rescue and Tragedy
in Scotland

PAUL HARRIS

The cockpit section of Flight PA 103, Tundergarth Hill,
December 23 1988.

The Scotsman Publications Ltd
in association with
Archive Publications Ltd

First published in Great Britain 1989 by
Archive Publications Ltd
10 Seymour Court
Manor Park
Runcorn
Cheshire

in association with

The Scotsman Publications Ltd
North Bridge
Edinburgh

Text and arrangement
© Copyright Archive Publications Ltd., 1989
Photographs © Copyright contributors, 1989 (see Sources page 128)

ISBN 0 948946 46 6 Hardback
ISBN 0 948946 45 8 Paperback

Also by Paul Harris and published by
Archive Publications

Edinburgh Since 1900
Aberdeen Since 1900
Edinburgh: The Fabulous Fifties
Aberdeen at War
Glasgow at War
Tyneside at War (with Clive Hardy)
By Appointment: Balmoral & Royal Deeside in Pictures

4. The Rosebank area of Lockerbie, December 23 1988.

CONTENTS

ACKNOWLEDGEMENTS

Many of the incidents described in this book have, up to now, only been alluded to in contemporary newspaper reports and, therefore, much of this information has derived from accounts printed in sources such as *The Scotsman* and *The Evening News*. Where I have drawn upon information in less ephemeral sources, these are acknowledged either in the text or in the Bibliography (page 126). The photographs are drawn for the mainpart from the files of The Scotsman Publications Ltd., but other sources are acknowledged on page 128.

I am particularly grateful to Brenda Woods and her staff at the library at *The Scotsman*; to Bill Brady for his advice and for printing the glass plates at *The Scotsman*; to Stuart Boyd, Picture Editor of *The Scotsman*; to Jim Seaton, News Editor of *The Scotsman;* to Ken Laird, assistant editor at the *Daily Record,* and to editor Endell Laird for their invaluable help with photographic material in colour available only from the *Record* archives; to Cyril Rice, Chief Librarian at *The Daily Record & Sunday Mail*; to Harry Roulston, Editor, and to Tommy Forsyth at the library of the *Press & Journal,* Aberdeen; to 'veteran' editor Clive Sandground for comments and reminiscences; to David Tinch, The Orkney Library; to Andrew Williamson, Curator, Shetland Museum; to Robert Wishart at *The Shetland Times*; to J Geddes Wood, Scotpix, Aberdeen; to John Mackinnon, Stornoway; to Tom Kidd; to Alex Duncan, Aberdeen; to staff at the Scottish section and Reference Library, Edinburgh District Libraries at George IV Bridge; to the Carnegie Library, Ayr; to The Mary Evans Picture Library, London; to Robin Bryden of Lockerbie; to the Imperial War Museum, London; to Mike Ashworth at The Scottish Mining Museum, Newtongrange; and to Clive Hardy for sharing his detailed knowledge of matters naval.

Finally, a note concerning the genesis of this book. This book was commissioned in November 1988, a full month before Lockerbie, and does not, therefore, represent a reaction to what was to be Scotland's worst disaster for more than a century. That there is enormous public interest in almost every aspect of accident and disaster is irrefutable: it has ever been thus and most recent newspaper and media coverage has continued to confirm this. It is very rarely, however, that such events are considered in the context of similar occurrences in history. The object of this book is, as factually as possible, in words and pictures, to introduce a new perspective and, maybe, shed a little light on the causes of, and contributory factors in, catastrophes from which , ultimately, none of us enjoy any guarantee of exemption. History *does* tend to repeat itself and some understanding of what has gone before is an essential prerequisite in preventing repetition.

Paul Harris
May 1989

INTRODUCTION

"In the year of our redemption 1097 . . . the land of Moray in Scotland . . . was desolated by the sea, castles subverted from the foundation, some towns destroyed, and the labours of man laid waste, by the discharge of sand by the sea; monstrous thunders also roaring, horrible and vast."

Hector Boece

Reading newspapers today, you might be forgiven for thinking that disasters are peculiarly modern occurences — connected with rail, air and road travel, the ravages of fire, earthquake, flood and suchlike, and exacerbated in effect by the incompetence of man. There is usually little historical perspective on the subject. Yet terrible disasters — both natural and man-made — have been visited upon humanity since the beginning of time itself. The great storms of wind, rain and sand of which Boece writes were not a new phenomenon, even in 1097. The prehistoric Stone Age village of Skara Brae in Orkney bears all the indications of having been overwhelmed by a sudden catastrophe which forced the inhabitants to flee: treasured possessions were abandoned, necklaces broken and beads scattered in the rush to evacuate, and the storerooms were deserted intact. But the village was not pillaged by foreign invaders. Modern archaeologists instead found the huts and passages choked with sand, evidence of a great storm which must have set the surrounding sand dunes in motion and induced a great and wholly unexpected panic.

Today man has learned to live with the elements.

Fortunately, great sandstorms like those at Skara Brae and the Culbin Sands of Moray in 1694 are no longer a threat, but wind, sea and snow are still largely untamed. Man's ability to actually provoke disaster has increased immeasurably. War, explosion, plane crashes, fire and collision of one sort or another are all precipitated by the agency of man as a result of his apparently increased sophistication and technical skills. Whilst we can only imagine for ourselves these disasters of the dim and distant past, those of the last century are made somewhat more accessible through the agency of the photograph or engraving.

For a variety of what seem to be totally unconnected reasons, there have been a quite extraordinary number of disasters — both natural and man-made — in the last one hundred years in Scotland, a relatively small country, and these have given birth to some stark and dramatic photographs. From early postcard views of the the Gretna rail crash (1915), Britain's worst ever railway accident, to the dramatic news photographs of Piper Alpha and the Lockerbie Boeing 747 disaster (1988), respectively the world's worst oilrig disaster and Britain's worst aviation disaster, the abilities of Scottish news photographers have all too regularly been put to the test over the years.

The climate and extensive coastline of this exposed northern European country have contributed to a whole series of maritime accidents. There have been the worst lifeboat disasters in Europe: at Arbroath, Broughty Ferry, Longhope

5. A dramatic contemporary picture postcard view of the disastrous fire at the Peebles Hydro Hotel, July 1905.

6. A Grampian Television E N G crew films the fire at Aberdeen Grammar School, July 1986.

and, thrice, at Fraserburgh lifeboat crews have been mourned. The main artery flowing between the Atlantic and North Seas — the notorious Pentland Firth — has been a graveyard for shipping since man set sail on the seas. And the indigenous fishing industry has provided more than its fair share of sacrifice in the cause of the breakfast kipper.

The decaying industrial heartland of Scotland has provided a backdrop for some devastating industrial accidents: mine disasters, explosions and fires. Glasgow, once the second city of the Empire, has seen its mouldering tenements and Victorian factories turn into deathtraps in time of fire, consuming workers and firemen alike in dramatic blazes like those at the Cheapside whisky bond and James Watt Street warehouse. The coming of the offshore oil industry to Scotland brought its own particular hazards alongside the particular urgency which it demands from all who serve it.

Domestically, it is difficult to explain the extraordinary number of fatal house fires which occur in Scotland: quite recently, it was revealed that Scotland enjoys the dubious distinction of one of the worst records in the world. It is unduly trite to ascribe this to "the Saturday night booze and chip pan phenomenon," heard recently from a blase old hand in the press corps. There is still a considerable amount of sub-standard housing stock and, until comparatively recently, the promotion of safety standards has been half-hearted, to put it mildly. It is only as recently as 1988 that smoke alarms have been actively promoted, following a series of house fires involving multiple fatalities.

The First and Second World Wars brought their own particular brands of tragedy — in the case of the latter, this came in the form of attack from the air and, in the former conflict, there was a series of disastrous maritime accidents with the sinking of HMS *Vanguard* in Scapa Flow, HMS *Natal* in the Cromarty Firth, HMS *Hampshire* off the Brough of Birsay, the so-called 'Battle of May Island' and the loss of the naval yacht *Iolaire* off Lewis. Ultimately, then, there was the loss of the entire German High Seas Fleet in the anchorage at Scapa.

The relative inaccessibility of Scottish targets with associated long flying times and their unconcentrated nature, spared Scotland from the persistent attentions of the Luftwaffe, although there were, of course, serious attacks from time to time, like those on Glasgow and Clydebank (March 1941), Greenock (May 1941) and Aberdeen (April 1943). This book does not deal extensively with the Second War period which has been dealt with in two other books (*Glasgow at War* by Paul Harris, 1986, and *Aberdeen at War* by Paul Harris, 1987); there is also the forthcoming *Scotland at War* by Ian Nimmo.

The capture of dramatic images of disasters poses its own particular range of challenges. The work of the photographer is normally uncomfortable and, frequently, downright dangerous. Just occasionally, a lucky frame will capture a disaster as it happens or very shortly afterwards (like the

Fraserburgh lifeboat going over) but usually the pictures which jump from the page over tea and marmalade in the morning are the result of long and distinctly unglamorous waiting about in rain, wind or snow: the waiting for survivors to appear at pithead or pierhead; for victims to be unearthed or revealed by lengthy search; for ships to be towed in, or for that rare image of an anguished face which says it all. As the Picture Editor on every newspaper knows, one good picture is better than a thousand words of journalistic copy.

Modern portable 35mm. cameras with electronic motor winds and rapid focussing and exposure techniques do render the capture of these images much easier. Until the early 1960s press photographers were still using cumbersome and slow plate cameras which, although they produced superb, sharp photographs from the large-format glass plates, meant that there was often only one try at that fleeting image. There simply was not the time to hang around and take another picture. Similarly, flash units were not of the instantly electronically-recharged equipment available today — after his initial attempt the photographer was obliged to wait patiently for the flash to recharge, often from heavy lead acid batteries. Early electronic flash units were widely distrusted — many photographers received nasty high voltage shocks using them — and bulb flash was extensively used by press photographers right into the '60s. This source of light was harsh and, used with high contrast press plates, the foreground blanched out if

the photographer was unlucky and, again, the camera did not have the same depth of field as its modern counterpart. Focussing was critical and it was not always possible to use a rangefinder: the art of the accurate 'guesstimate' was an essential prerequisite in the press photographer. All this taken into consideration, many of the pictures reproduced in this book represent a not inconsiderable tribute to the skill of the photographers involved.

Skill is not the only vital component in many of these pictures. The situations in which press photographers find themselves very often demand a very considerable amount of physical courage. Clive Sandground, then an assistant editor on the *Scottish Daily Express*, remembers the night of the Cheapside whisky bond fire in 1960, when every available fire appliance in Glasgow fought the conflagration. "The heat was so intense that, at first, our photographers couldn't get within half a mile of the fire. At great personal risk they eventually got to the fire and were there as the walls of the warehouse collapsed onto the firemen. The photographers were lucky to be alive."

For Sandground, the Cheapside fire brought home "the power of black and white pictures used *big* . . . we used page after page of them right through the paper and as more came in we revamped the paper right through the night, printing late editions right up to seven in the morning."

Almost invariably, on a major news story involving human tragedy, there are moral dilemnas affecting both journalist and photographer. There is

7. Artist Ian Fleming's oil painting of the rescue of survivors from the Maryhill tenement collapse following the air raid of March 14 1941.

8. "For those in peril on the sea!" An early postcard, circa 1900, published in Edinburgh, and depicting an old Scottish pulling lifeboat.

a thin dividing line between servicing the public interest and the display of what might be perceived as being in bad taste. I can recall, in the late 1960s, seeing photographers turn away from the tearful bereaved, cameras silent, with the grim, simple observation, "Private grief". I am dubious as to whether similar scenes evoke the same response today in a world more hardened to tragedy and suffering: in a world where the reading and viewing public are more accustomed to a detailed and intimate outpouring of tragedy, especially on television. Not that the competition for the story or the picture was any less in, say, the '50s or '60s. The job of the journalist or photographer, in the wake of tragedy, has always been a distasteful one and recent disasters have sparked controversy over the ways in which news and pictures are brought to the public. Some of the most successful of news photographers and journalists possess a talent for easy bonhommie and comforting familiarity — comforting, that is to say, to persons newly bereaved or affected by tragedy and who often wish to actually communicate to someone their experience. The denizens of the press, though, are not necessarily the best people to unburden ones soul to although they may appear attentive listeners. And comparatively few people tend to like to read what later appears — even in their own daily newspaper.

In his autobiography, *A Grain of Truth*, one of Scotland's most respected (and respectable) journalists, Jack Webster, writes of the aftermath of the 1953 Fraserburgh lifeboat disaster: "That evening I had the melancholy task of visiting the homes of the dead to collect photographs and biographical details for the next day's *Press & Journal*...". At least Jack would have turned a sympathetic ear and returned the photographs after use, unlike some relentless characters who would have the family snaps cleared from the dresser in the time it takes to brew a cup of tea. Regrettably or otherwise, there has always been a general interest on the part of members of the human species in the misfortunes of their brothers and sisters — and the press at least partially exists to service that morose interest. The moral issue does not really revolve around this point but rather around the manner in which newspapers operate.

No two journalists — never mind members of the public — are likely to agree on what constitutes 'responsible' journalism and newspaper readers are only too well aware of how different newspapers are likely to treat the same story. How it is treated is, of course, no longer of any account to the deceased victims of tragedy but it is, rather, the bereaved who carry the burden of anguish and who stand to be adversely affected by insensitive newspaper treatment. Nevertheless, as early as the turn of the century photographers were turning a penny by capturing images of train crashes, disastrous fires and other accidents.

Up until the end of the First World War, most of the photographs of disasters and other newsworthy events were not, in fact, taken by press photographers but by local photographers living in the area of an incident. The technology did not exist at that time for introducing these images into the breakfast-time newspaper context: most daily newspapers contained few — if any — photographs. By the end of the first decade of the century, weekly magazines like *The Illustrated London News* and *The Graphic*, which had hitherto featured engravings and drawings of major disasters, were printing photographs. There was a definite hunger on the part of the public for a photographic record of dreadful events and many local photographers, perceiving the market which was largely unsatisfied, issued their best photographs as postcards, in whatever quantity the market dictated. Thus, many thousands of copies of the many postcards of an incident like the Gretna rail disaster (1915) were printed and sold; an incident which, by its very scale had commmanded wide public attention. On the other hand, only a few hundred would probably have been made of the Fife railway disaster (1914) or the Elliott Junction collision at Arbroath (1906).

Similarly, there were many different views and representations of the big fire at the Peebles Hydropathic Hotel in 1905, produced commercially in enormous quantities, but the image of the fire at Mugdrum House in Fife (1916), printed as a real photograph, bears the appearance of a postcard produced for a strictly limited local circulation by Robertson Bros. of Newburgh.

"Hold the front page!" is the traditional shout of the shirt-sleeved, green eyeshade-sporting newspaper editor cast in the Hollywood mould. It is a dramatic image in itself that of a great newspaper about to run on the presses and suddenly and unexpectedly grinding to a halt as word of a big story filters in at deadline time. As the story breaks in the newsroom, reporters hit the telephones, copy boys dash downstairs bearing dramatic stories to the linotype operators who set them in hot metal and, late but up to the minute, the great presses start to roll throwing out freshly printed pages hot off the press and heavily perfumed with printers' ink . . .

Well, that is the image which may be conjured up in the mind but, in reality, things never were and most certainly are not like that today. Journalists who have worked fifty years in the business cannot remember an editor emerging from his office and barking the magic command. And, besides, many newspapers, including *The Scotsman* and *The Evening News*, have only comparatively recently taken classified advertisements off that very front page (the former paper in 1957 and the latter a few years later). The highly conservative D C Thomson daily publication the *Courier and Advertiser*, Dundee's morning paper, announced only in December 1988 that the classified advertisements were to disappear from the front page.

The much vaunted new technology which has transformed the British newspaper industry has itself changed newspaper practices for ever. Battered old

typewriters in the newsroom have been replaced by computer terminals where stories are directly inputted by the journalists for transformation into type. The noisy clattering linotype machines in the basement have, most likely, been replaced by a smoothly humming master computer which controls the whole operation. In fact, the last newspaper in Scotland to use the traditional method of printing and typesetting, *The Inverness Courier*, abandoned it and switched to computers in October 1988. Newsrooms are now somewhat quieter, lower key establishments where neat young men brought up in the age of the computer tap away at their terminals in a completely changed world from that perhaps somewhat romanticised one where some drunken old hack, complete with hat and overcoat, bashes away at the reluctant keys of an ageing typewriter.

The relatively recent advent of colour printing in the newspaper industry has placed new demands upon both photographer and reproductive technology. The *Daily Record* was still coming to grips with the then highly innovative and complex technology associated with colour reproduction in October 1971, following its move from Hope Street to new, modern premises at Anderston Quay, when the news of the Clarkston gas explosion broke. Launch date for colour production was still a full month off, but an editorial and management decision was immediately reached to bring plans forward and feature this dramatic story in full colour on the front page the next day.

Scottish Daily Express editor at the time was Clive Sandground who recalls, "When we saw the front page of the *Record* the day after the Clarkston disaster we knew the writing was on the wall for the *Express* in Scotland . . .". Although the *Express* had been using colour for some time for advertising features, printed in Peterborough, senior editorial staff and Sandground, in particular, felt that the looming circulation war would be won by the newspaper which switched to colour on editorial pages. When the *Record* left Hope Street it was selling around 400,000 copies a day and the *Scottish Daily Express* 620,000. Within a month of the dramatic Clarkston colour front page the *Record* was up to around 550,000 and the skids were under the *Express* circulation. The *Record* had, in fact, pulled off a remarkable coup which even Fleet Street had not thus far dared attempt with what was seen at the time as unreliable, if not downright unworkable, modern technology. And not only was that coup pulled off a full month ahead of schedule, but it was all effectively organised in the course of a single working day. The *Record* was on its way to becoming Scotland's bestselling daily newspaper and the *Scottish Daily Express* pulled down the shutters in Scotland just over two years later in March 1974. In May of that year, Jocelyn Stevens

9. The historic *Daily Record* colour front page of the Clarkston disaster, October 22 1971.

10. On the spot colour news photograph of the Grosvenor Hotel, Glasgow, on the *Sunday Mail* front page January 8, 1978.

11. Reporting the disaster on *Piper Alpha*, July 8 1988.

observed from his hot seat at the head of the Beaverbrook group: "We employ too many people and pay them too much money. At the maximum, we have two years in which to put our house in order . . .".

Recent developments in newspaper technology, allied to the breakdown of traditional labour and manning practices, pioneered by Eddy Shah and taken up enthusiastically by others, have dramatically lowered the circulation breakeven points on new titles and enabled regional printing to re-emerge in Scotland. Papers like the *Scottish Daily News* and *Sunday Standard*, casualties of the old-fashioned newspaper industry in the late 70s and early 80s, are now being successfully emulated, in technical terms, by *Scotland on Sunday*, and a myriad of free sheets.

Although the *Record* was actually the newspaper to pioneer the editorial use of colour in the UK, much of the credit tends to be popularly attributed to Shah's *Today* newspaper which was put together in London and then printed in the regions, thanks to modern technology and telephone based communications. The *Daily Post* launch was based on the same theory, only this time around Shah decided to attempt it from Warrington in Lancashire with associated lower overheads. Now, of course, the newspaper industry is fast reaching the situation where colour will be the norm rather than an exciting innovation.

The printing of Scottish editions of the *Express* and *Daily Mail*, abandoned by the *Express* in March 1974 and the *Mail* in 1967, has now been copied by titles as diverse as *The Sun* and *The Sunday Times*, printing out of Murdoch's Glasgow Kinning Park plant. In theory, this should mean that thorough and later coverage of Scottish news stories is facilitated, although availability of printing technology is only one part of the equation: a newspaper also needs the experienced journalists and photographers on the ground to bring the story to the readers. In a major disaster situation being able to put the troops in in sufficient numbers, and to keep them there, is vital. A case in point was the Ibrox disaster — within a matter of hours the *Scottish Daily Express* had pulled their men in from all over Scotland and had almost 100 journalists and photographers on the story. The paper the next day bore the evidence of their efforts. One *Express* staff man at the time recalls, "I think we got a 'collect' picture of every single victim." With 69 dead that represented a lot of legwork.

More recently, the Lockerbie disaster in December 1988 was a very real test of newspaper expertise. The story broke just after 7.00 in the evening in Edinburgh and Glasgow with telephone calls from local Lockerbie freelances when front pages were already planned, and on a day shortly before Christmas when a certain degree of relaxation

had set in in the newsroom — indeed, in one case, in the middle of the Christmas party. With only three hours or so before first editions were to print, it was necessary to get journalists and photographers to a relatively remote part of Scotland with the connecting trunk road — the A74 — impassable with wreckage, other roads choked with traffic, police turning back cars headed to Lockerbie (including journalists), power lines down and communications links severed. Stories had to be filed, pictures got back to the office and Scottish sub-editors had to virtually lay out completely new papers.

For any newspaper, dealing with a major disaster story like this represents an enormous impromptu challenge. The scenario cannot be rehearsed. In *The Scotsman* newsroom the first inkling of the story came shortly after 7p.m. with a call from the home of a local Lockerbie photographer: the first of a series of conflicting reports. It was thought then that possibly a light aircraft had crashed in the area and more information was awaited. Shortly afterwards, came another call, this one anonymous, saying that a jet had crashed and had hit a petrol station. At that stage there was some speculation as to whether the British Airways Shuttle flight from Heathrow had gone down. And then came another report that a mid-air collision had occurred. *The Scotsman*, had by now despatched its Glasgow news editor and two others from the Glasgow office to Lockerbie and Magnus Linklater, *Scotsman* editor, had abandoned a black tie dinner party he was attending, given by the managing director of The Scotsman Publications Ltd., and was heading back to the office to personally take charge of the fast developing situation. The firm news that Pan Am flight PA 103 was down on Lockerbie came around 7.45p.m. on the newsroom teletext screen and a car left Edinburgh to assist with coverage. News editor Seaton decided to put "a small efficient team" into the story rather than trying to flood Lockerbie with men. "I knew the police would be sealing off Lockerbie — and, indeed, our Glasgow team had some difficulty getting through the police roadblock on the A74 — and I also realised that the best stuff would be coming from the local men who were already there, on the ground". That having been said, that night, virtually every off-duty reporter on the paper 'phoned and offered to come in and help on the story. By now, reams of information were flowing off the Press Association tapes, originating from the local 'stringers', and Seaton deputed James Meek to pull the story together from all the reports, with rewrites and updates for each edition. At 3 a.m., for example, a dramatic report came from the Glasgow team who had discovered the wreckage of the nose cone section at Tundergarth Hill, three miles outside Lockerbie. *The Scotsman* kept printing right through to a later than usual last edition at 4 a.m.

Over the next couple of weeks, *The Scotsman* kept a maximum of just four journalists on the story at any one time and, so far as possible, kept the same reporters and photographers on the story. This was probably the key to its successful in-depth coverage. "We felt that a small team would achieve more than the sort of large team put in by some of the tabloids — the men in large teams tend to end up competing against each other," observed a senior member of the editorial team. That having been said, although he feels that the large teams were largely self-defeating, he takes the view that the tabloids, by and large, handled the story "very professionally — for the first time for a long time they had a *real* story to get their teeth into rather than a piece of trivia".

By January 4, the day of the Memorial Service, the paper was aware, however, that "Lockerbie had had enough of us — the sheer number of press hunting in packs rather than the stories produced — had wearied the people there". The next day, after one of the local funerals, *The Scotsman* pulled photographers and journalists out "to leave Lockerbie in peace," and returned only once in the following month for an official press conference given by the Chief Constable.

The varying performances of the Scottish papers are, perhaps, interesting to note. The English papers, of course, missed out on pictures the next morning — with the exception of library pics of Boeing 747s — as did the *Scottish Daily Express*, printed in Manchester. Both the *Sun*, benefiting from printing in Glasgow, and the *Daily Record* carried several pages of dramatic pictures. The early editions of the *Record* had pictures in black and white only but the later ones were carrying colour taken at Lockerbie only hours previously. *The Scotsman* coverage was particularly good with three pages of stories and pictures, enhanced by the paper's broadsheet format.

The second day of newspaper coverage was not so much a test of fast response ability as a reflection of "troops on the ground" as every British newspaper — and many foreign ones — poured journalists and photographers into the little market town of Lockerbie. The coverage on Friday December 23 was intensive (one tabloid newspaper

12. Robin Bryden, a photographer based in Lockerbie, was the first press photographer on the scene following the crash of Pan Am Flight PA103 on the town. This photograph, of houses burning in Sherwood Crescent, was taken minutes after the crash.

carried 15 bylines) and, inevitably, those newspapers with colour printing facilities scored heavily: both the *Daily Record* and *Today* used wraparound front to back page colour pictures of the crashed nose section of the 747, the latter's layout scoring somewhat higher points. The stark quality of black and white photographs are particularly graphic in the context of a major disaster and *The Scotsman* and *Daily Telegraph* maximised in this area. Their larger broadsheet page size also gave them an advantage over the tabloids with dramatic pictures used over the width of the page.

By the Saturday, day three of the story, the in-depth assessments and 'collect' pictures were making their appearance. This was still a very big story — one which, in the parlance of the business, would "run and run" — and this was the last major crack at it for the press before Christmas. But the most dramatic of the pictures had by now been used and only the more macabre and maudlin aspects remained: recovery of the bodies, anguished relatives and the heartbreak of Christmas Day services turned into occasions of remembrance rather than celebration. In fact, the story did run as a very major one until the Memorial Service at Dryfesdale Church (January 4) and the first local funerals the following day, although, by that time, a very definite local reaction was setting in against the media "circus". As Erlend Clouston of *The Guardian* put it, "one person's professional zeal is another person's bad taste."

By and large, the British press exhibited reasonable taste in what was printed in terms of both words and pictures. The Continental press, by contrast, used considerably more harrowing pictures: Spanish and German news magazines gave their readers the dubious benefit of images of bodies being removed from the roofs of houses in Lockerbie.

The Dumfries & Galloway police unofficially estimate that in excess of 1,000 journalists, photographers and TV personnel flooded into the little town of Lockerbie in the week after the disaster. There were TV crews from as far away as Belgium, Luxembourg, France, Mexico, Brazil, Japan, Australia, the United States and, even, Fiji: two crews attended from Rupert Murdoch's satellite based Sky Channel which was not even on the air at that stage.

The vast number of journalists put on the story by the news desks meant that every newspaper was able to cover Britain's worst aviation disaster — and Scotland's worst disaster for more than 100 years — in considerable depth and from every imaginable angle: from eye witness accounts, assessments of possible causes and impact upon the bereaved to long term effects on the community. The terrorist implications of the disaster served to put an even greater international perspective and importance upon one of the greatest news stories of the century. When the confirmation eventually came on December 28 that the crash was caused by a terrorist bomb (*The Times* did, in fact, announce this unofficially from unconfirmed reports that morning), it was, significantly, announced by the senior crash investigator at a news conference convened in Lockerbie. The story was still very much centred on the Borders town.

Inevitably, the Lockerbie disaster was rendered even more poignant by its occurrence just before Christmas and New Year, traditionally a time for peace, goodwill and celebration. Over the years it seems that this time of the year is all too regularly marred by the tragic: December 1988 had already been marked by the railway accident at Clapham and, abroad, the earthquake in Armenia. This is not a new perception. The editorial in *The Scotsman* of Wednesday, January 1 1930, the day after the Paisley cinema fire in which 70 children died, noted: "It is a melancholy circumstance that the close of the year has been clouded in Scotland by what must be regarded as one of the most poignant disasters on record. Such occurrences all too regularly attend upon the Christmas and New Year period. They have arisen generally from railway accidents, due to the complications of handling a heavy rush of traffic, or from shipwrecks, occasioned by the stormy seas which are common at this time of the year. The Paisley disaster, however, is a reminder that there are other forms of terror lurking in the conditions of modern existence . . .".

That same editorial might have been published almost word for word the day after the Lockerbie disaster with the simple substitution of a different placename. And, to pile disaster upon disaster, on January 8 1989 a Boeing 737 of British Midland Airways was to crash at East Midlands Airport whilst attempting an emergency landing after the

13. Lockerbie: one of the biggest news stories of the 20th century. How different newspapers reported the story: *The Scotsman* of December 22, Edinburgh *Evening News* of December 22, *Today* of December 23 and *Daily Record* of December 23 1988.

THE SCOTSMAN

No. 45,337   4 a.m. news   **Thursday, December 22, 1988**   Price 30p

A town laid waste

Daily Record
22p   FORWARD WITH SCOTLAND

276 DEAD
SCOTLAND'S BIGGEST TRAGEDY...

WARNED
— BUT AIRLINE KEPT BOMB THREAT SECRET

LOCKERBIE AIR DISASTER...Pages 2 and 3 ● Pages 4 and 5 ● Pages 6 and 7 ● Pages 8 and 9 ● Centre Pages

EDITION

Evening News

No 36,026   PRICE 20p   Tel 031-225 2468   ★   **THURSDAY, DECEMBER 22, 1988**

THEN THE DAWN

Today
NEWSPAPER OF THE YEAR

END OF FLIGHT 103
STRUCK DOWN IN COLD BLOOD

port engine caught fire: 46 passengers were to die after the aircraft crashed onto the embankment at the side of the M1 motorway.

Every major accident or disaster produces a similar aftermath: questions, recrimination and an enquiry of one sort or another. After due deliberation and the weighing of an often formidable quantity of evidence, an official report is issued. But just as surely as this procedure unfolds, there is another accident waiting to happen . . . . And when that does happen, the press are just as surely there to cover it in words and pictures, feeding the appetite of the public. The pattern continues. Then, in Jack Lemmon's words in Billy Wilder's classic film *The Front Page*, "Next day somebody wraps a front page around a mackerel."

BIBLIOGRAPHY

BOOKS

Ansdell, I, et. al.: *Scottish Shipwreck & Disaster Stories*, Newtongrange 1984
Chambers, Robert: *Notices of the Most Remarkable Fires in Edinburgh*, Edinburgh 1824
Cornell, James: *The Great International Disaster Book*, New York 1976
The Daily Record & Sunday Mail: *Front Page Scotland*, Glasgow 1988
Duckham, Helen & Baron: *Great Pit Disasters, Great Britain 1700 to the Present Day*, Newton Abbot, 1973
Dyall, Valentine: *Famous Sea Tragedies*, London 1955
Farr, A Derek: *Let Not the Deep: The Story of the RNLI*, Aberdeen 1973
Ferguson, David M: *Shipwrecks of Orkney, Shetland and the Pentland Firth*, Newton Abbot 1988
Gilding, Laurence F: *The Book of Sea Rescue*, London 1964
Haine, Edgar A: *Disaster at Sea*, New York 1983
O'Hare, Larry: *The Stanrigg Pit Disaster*, Monkland, 1987
Harris, Paul: *Aberdeen at War*, Aberdeen & Manchester 1987
Harris, Paul: *Glasgow at War*, Glasgow & Manchester 1986
Hocking, Charles: *Dictionary of Disasters at Sea During the Age of Steam 1824 - 1962*, London 1969
Jones, Fred: *Air Crash: The Clues in the Wreckage*, London 1985
Kerr, J Lennox: *The Great Storm*, London 1954
McKee, Alexander: *Black Saturday: The Tragedy of the Royal Oak*, London 1959
Masters, David: *When Ships Go Down: More Wonders of Salvage*, London, 1945 edn.
Masters, David: *Wonders of Salvage*, London 1946 edn.
Nock, O S: *Historic Railway Disasters*, London 1966
Octopus Books: *The World's Worst Disasters of the 20th Century*, London 1984
Rolt, L T C: *Red for Danger: A History of Railway Accidents and Railway Safety*, Newton Abbot, revised 4th edn. 1986
Scarlett, Bernard: *Shipminder: The Story of Her Majesty's Coastguard*, London 1971
Stewart, Stanley: *Air Disasters*, London 1988 edn.
Swinson, Arthur: *Scotch on the Rocks*, London 1963
Vat, D van der: *The Grand Scuttle: The Sinking of the German Fleet at Scapa Flow in 1919*, London 1982
Weaver, H J: *Nightmare at Scapa Flow: The Truth about the Sinking of H M S Royal Oak*, London 1980
Webb, William: *Coastguard: An Official History of H M Coastguard*, London 1976
Webster, Jack: *A Grain of Truth: A Scottish Journalist Remembers*, Edinburgh 1981
White, John Baker: *Sabotage is Suspected*, London 1957

NEWSPAPERS

The Scotsman, Edinburgh
The Evening News, Edinburgh
The Evening Dispatch, Edinburgh
The Daily Record, Glasgow
The Sunday Mail, Glasgow
The Shetland Times, Lerwick
The Orcadian, Kirkwall

SEA

14. Heading for home. An Aberdeen trawler tries to make it into harbour.

Scotland's extensive and exposed coastline has led to much loss of life at sea, local vessels and unwary visitors suffering alike in storms like the one above: this photograph showing a trawler attempting to round the south breakwater and find the sanctuary of Aberdeen harbour in March 1969 was reproduced on front pages all over the world. Many fishing communities have suffered losses on a catastrophic scale which have certainly not arisen from any lack of respect for the elements — simply the impossibility of predicting them. Without the advantage of either barometer or weather forecasts, sudden storms caught whole fishing fleets thirty or forty miles out, as on July 16 1832 when 31 Shetland 'sixerns' were lost together with 105 crewmen. To this day the event is remembered simply as 'The Bad Day'. Also off Shetland, ten boats and 58 men were lost on July 20 1881.

In the same year there was the loss of almost half the Eyemouth fishing fleet on October 14 1881. When the fleet sailed that morning, the sun was shining and although the glass was falling the sea was calm and the wind still. But at midday the weather changed with terrifying suddenness: the skies went black, a ferocious gale blew up and the seas boiled up in a frenzy. Some boats capsized and sank immediately, others were cast onto the rocks in their attempts to reach the refuge of harbour. The force of the gale was such that those ashore were barely able to stand, let alone launch rescue attempts. Other boats were driven ashore at Burnmouth, Berwick and Goswick. For four days battered fishing boats from the scattered fleet turned up at ports as far away as South Shields but, of the 45 which sailed, only 26 returned. On that day of sudden and unpredictable storm 189 fishermen were lost — 129 of them from Eyemouth. Only 30 bodies were ever recovered. One in three of the town's fishermen died in the great storm of Black Friday and the fishing industry there was devastated.

A dramatic and significant disaster which occurred on July 3 1883 involving the S S *Daphne* actually took place no further out to sea than Linthouse on the Clyde when the ill fated coaster rolled over and sank on launching. No less than 124 shipyard workers on board lost their lives. The commission which was set up to investigate the accident concluded that shipyards were, in fact, taking too little account of safety in design and general seaworthiness of the vessels they were building and shipbuilders, as a direct result, began to invest more heavily in research and safety techniques.

There have been a number of periods when sustained bad weather off the Scottish coasts has brought about a series of casualties — such as in the period October—December 1959. In that December the gales raged for ten days without abating resulting in the loss of 27 lives. The casualty board at Lloyds in London was unable to list all the ships in trouble. On Sunday December 6 winds reached Force 15—110 m.p.h. — which is virtually unheard of around the British coasts. Over the next three days there was much rescue and tragedy involving the *George Robb*, *Servus*, *Anna*, North Carr Light Vessel and Broughty Ferry lifeboat.

There had been a similar period at the end of January 1953 when a period of sustained high winds combined with a particularly high tide occasioned havoc throughout Britain. The most serious casualty was the loss of the car and passenger ferry *Princess Victoria* en route from Stranraer to Larne, but there were many other casualties including the stranding of the 7000-ton freighter *Clan Macquarrie* at Borve, the disappearance of the Grimsby trawler *Sheldon* off Orkney, the loss of the trawler *Michael Griffith* with all 14 hands off Barra Head and the loss of two crewmen from the Islay lifeboat going to the rescue of the last casualty. As the period of storm stretched into February, the casualties increased and by the time the Great Storm, as it became known, had blown itself out after four days more than 300 lives had been lost at sea in over 50 separate incidents.

Most of the more serious lifeboat disasters in Britain have taken place off the coasts of north and east Scotland: three times involving the Fraserburgh lifeboat and once each involving the Arbroath, Broughty Ferry and Longhope lifeboats. The loss of the last Fraserburgh lifeboat was less than a year after the loss of the Longhope lifeboat and grave doubts were being expressed about lifeboat policy and design. Thus the results of enquiries into the Fraserburgh disaster were awaited with more than the usual degree of interest. Unlike Longhope, on this occasion there was the evidence of both an actual photograph and witnesses aboard the *Opal* and a Russian factory ship.

The official Department of Trade enquiry concluded: "... the lifeboat was struck by a very large breaking wave fine on her port bow and was overwhelmed by that wave.

It appears that the bow was lifted high into the air and the vessel capsized bow over stern with some transverse inclination to starboard and lay capsized . . .". The formal investigation under the Merchant Shipping Act (1891) came up with one particularly sensible conclusion: "Lifeboats . . . must be available for rescue in inshore waters and at some considerable distance from shore . . . too much is expected of the majority of lifeboats. Most of those now in service are designed for work both close inshore and further afield. Their shallow draught entails tunnel screws and the corresponding hull forms have comparatively poor resistance and propulsion qualities . . . For what may be termed deep sea work, craft of greater size and displacement are desirable if lifeboats are to survive the frequent, severe North Sea storm conditions . . . In the district around Peterhead one such large lifeboat could be available for distant work, with smaller boats for inshore rescues." The suggestion of a 70 foot boat for the area around Fraserburgh would certainly seem to have been eminently sensible — the problem being that a boat of such size would not have been able to get in and out of the harbour in all states of weather and tide. In the following years, however, more sophisticated lifeboat designs were brought into production by the RNLI including the new 50-foot Thames Class of steel lifeboat and increased use of the larger Clyde class boats.

In recent years improved facilities for helicopter rescue have benefited seafarers around Scottish coasts. After the loss of the fishing boat *Bon Ami* with all six of her crew off the west coast of Scotland near Lochinver in 1985, it became apparent that a serious gap existed in search and rescue services. In optimum weather the fastest time a helicopter could reach many parts of the west coast from RAF Lossiemouth was 90 minutes and in bad weather, if a detour was required around Cape Wrath or through the Great Glen, the time was often considerably longer. After the loss of the *Bon Ami* an official hearing in Inverness recommended the establishment of a search and rescue (SAR) helicopter at Stornoway. Bristows now operate the SAR helicopters for the Coastguard at Stornoway — and at Sumburgh in Shetland. In its first 18 months of operation the Stornoway base was credited with the saving of no less than 97 lives at a time when there were more maritime casualties than ever off the west coast of Scotland, due to a pronounced increase in coastal traffic in the area. (In fact, the lifeboat station at Oban is now the second busiest in the whole of the UK — second only to that on the Humber which is the country's only fully manned station.) In 1988, Stornoway coastguard handled 125% more casualties than in the previous year. The new helicopter service has not, however, been operated without a certain degree of cost over and above its basic £ 1,000 an hour: on November 8 1988 the Sikorsky S61N aircraft was forced to ditch in the Minch while proceeding to an emergency.

The need for rapid response to emergencies at sea is highlighted by the fact that the temperature of the seas around the north and west of Scotland severely limit survival times in the water. It has been calculated that there is a one in four chance of a maritime incident in these waters ending in fatality as opposed to a one in twenty-five chance elsewhere around the British coastline.

Most often, the first news of a casualty comes by radio and thus the alert to local coastguard, and then to lifeboat secretary, or other ships, derives initially from one of the coast radio stations located at Portpatrick, Oban, Wick and Stonehaven. These stations handle all the normal day to day radio traffic required by ships at sea — radio telephone calls to owners and relatives, weather forecasts, gale warnings and navigational warnings — as well as the more serious distress traffic. Rescue work is facilitated by the relaying of Mayday messages and information to other ships in the area of a casualty on the international distress frequency of 2182 kc/s. by the transmitters of the relatively powerful coast radio stations, which thereby provide a vital service.

Over the years, much life has been saved from ships driven ashore by the mechanism of the breeches buoy. It was invented, according to popular legend, by Admiral Lord Nelson but actually derived from a system devised by the little known eccentric George Manby (1765 — 1854) who, in 1808, saved six seamen near Yarmouth by the device of a rope attached to a shot fired from a mortar. The breeches buoy was taken out of service by the Department of Transport in 1988, having been condemned as out of date. Supporters, however, point out that there are instances in very strong winds on a lee shore when the admittedly more modern aid of the helicopter simply cannot be brought into use. The British equipment taken out of service was, however, eagerly snapped up by the Irish Rescue Service. The traditional British apparatus was abandoned against a background of cuts in the Coastguard service: in the late 1970s more than 700 full time coastguard officers worked in 28 stations around Britain. By Spring 1989 this had dropped to 538 in 21 centres, following the controversial closure of Scotland's Peterhead station which, it was reported, had been able to take over normal duties from coastguard headquarters at Aberdeen during the major incident caused by the Piper Alpha explosion.

Modern technology and the insatiable appetite of the internal combustion engine brought a new phenomenon to the waters around the Scottish coast in the early 1970s — the offshore oil rig. The planting of these enormous sophisticated structures in the unfriendly waters of the North Sea brought a whole series of new problems and dangers. Although accidents of one sort or another became accepted as everyday risks, it took a string of disasters to bring home the need for perpetual vigilance so far as safety was concerned. The Ekofisk blowout in 1977 was a harbinger of more serious incidents and the collapse of the accommodation rig *Alexander Keilland* in the Norwegian sector of the North Sea in March 1980 with the loss of 100 lives was, at the time, the worst accident to date. It was not until 1988 that the North Sea was to see what many thought had been on the cards for a long time with the horrific explosion and fire on *Piper Alpha*. A similar catastrophe was only narrowly averted a few months later on *Ocean Oddyssey* and then, on December 24 1988, the huge floating storage oil tanker *Fulmar FSU* broke free from its supposedly permanent mooring in the oilfield and actually drifted towards the neighbouring, manned Clyde production platform for almost an hour before the incident was noted. A collision between the two would, needless to say, have had disastrous consequences.

15. On July 3 1883 the *Daphne* capsized on launching from a Linthouse shipyard and 124 shipyard workers were drowned in the worst accident of its type ever experienced on the Clyde.

16. Grounding of *Nessmore* off Coll, November 20 1895

The *Nessmore* was en route from Montreal to Liverpool with cattle and general cargo when gales followed by thick fog caused her to stray from her set course. On the night of November 20 1895 she went aground on a reef half a mile offshore from the island of Coll. Most of the 550 head of cattle aboard swam ashore to Coll although some 'mysteriously' ended up on Tiree. There was a valuable general cargo of 4,000 tons also aboard and Lloyds underwriters, depicted in this contemporary engraving, despatched a number of steamers and tugs to take part in a difficult salvage operation, in the course of which the Salvage Assocation vessel *Hyaena* temporarily joined the casualty on the reef. The *Nessmore* became a total loss.

17, 18. Steamships *Stromboli* and *Kathleen* in collision, December 31 1904

On December 31 1904 the steamer *Stromboli*, outward bound for the Mediterranean, ran into the Glasgow steamer *Kathleen*, inward from Bilbao, off Garvel Point, Greenock, The *Kathleen* was carrying iron ore, the weight of which caused her to settle in the water very quickly as can be seen in these contemporary postcard views: two of her engineers drowned and traffic on the Clyde was considerably obstructed. The bows of the *Stromboli* were firmly wedged amidships of the other vessel and both settled together. The incident caused much excitement at the time, occurring as it did at such a busy point on the Clyde.

STEAMSHIPS "STROMBOLI" AND "KATHLEEN," SUNK BY COLLISION OFF GARVEL POINT, GREENOCK, 31ST DECEMBER, 1904, AS SEEN AT LOW WATER.

P. Anderson, Yr., Photo.

KATHLEEN

The Scaurs, Cruden Bay and Wreck Easdale.

19. Wreck of *Easdale* on The Scaurs, Cruden Bay

A pre-1914 postcard view of the coaster *Easdale* hard aground near Cruden Bay, Aberdeenshire, issued by the local chemist, William Bremner.

20. *Kathleen Annie,* stranded Eday, September 29 1924

The four-masted schooner *Kathleen Annie* stranded on the Green Holms, Eday, officially on passage from Bremen to Newfoundland with a cargo of 17,000 cases of rectified spirit. The schooner was later refloated and beached at Kirkwall but her condition was too far gone to save her and she was broken up. Her cargo was successfully salvaged although the steam drifter *Busy Bee* caught fire and sank during the course of the operation after the spirit leaked and the fumes were ingnited by cinders from the stoke hold. There were shades of 'Whisky Galore' (S S *Politician,* q.v.) when it was discovered by the authorities that some of the cargo had disappeared and it was dicovered that it was being used to pep up the local home brew of the islanders! It was suspected at the time that the cargo was in actuality destined for Prohibition era United States purchasers.

Torpedo Destroyer "Laverock,"

21. Torpedo destroyer *Laverock* **aground Skelmorlie, February 28 1914**

This (left) was one of a number of postcard views of the torpedo destroyer *Laverock* high and dry opposite Blackhouse by Skelmorlie, Ayrshire, in February 1914. This 260-foot long 'L' class destroyer was built on the Clyde by Yarrows and launched in November, 1913. On February 28 1914, she was running her trials on the Skelmorlie measured mile with a Clyde pilot on board when, as she turned, her steering gear failed to respond and she steamed hard aground. Her port bilge was ripped open and both propellors and rudder were torn off. As she was high and dry, the decision was made to repair her where she lay, which work is shown in this view, prior to floating her off.

22. *Celtic,* **wrecked Bay of Skaill, August 9 1907**

The barquentine *Celtic* was wrecked near Sandwick, Orkney, after suffering storm damage at sea and drifting ashore. Her damaged fore topmast can be seen in this photograph.

THE "BEN NAMUR" ASHORE AT BAY OF SKAILL, 10·10·20.

23. *Ben Namur* **Aground Bay of Skaill, Orkney, October 10 1920**
This dramatic photograph shows salvage operations on the Aberdeen trawler *Ben Namur*, stranded on the north side of the Bay of Skaill. She ran aground in thick fog and a heavy swell and the official inquiry found that the skipper had failed to establish his position before setting his course. All the crew with the exception of two washed overboard were saved after a line was floated ashore.

"St Sunniva" on Mousa.

24. *St. Sunniva (I)* **aground Mousa, April 10 1930**

The Aberdeen North of Scotland Steamship Company mail steamer *St. Sunniva (I)* shared a similar fate to the *St. Rognovald* after a previous escape from stranding. She ran aground in February 1914 near Graemeshall, Orkney en route from Aberdeen to Lerwick with passengers and cargo. She was successfully refloated on this occasion, later went aground near Peterhead in 1928 and finally came to grief on Mousa, Shetland, in thick fog on April 10 1930, en route from Kirkwall to Lerwick. The crew and 40 passengers reached Mousa in the ships' lifeboats. She broke up after a fortnight aground. It is interesting to note that much of the mail was lost and that thousands of pounds worth of payments to knitwear workers in Shetland were irretrievably lost, being in the form of postal orders.

25. Mail steamer *St. Rognovald* **aground Brough Head, Orkney, April 24 1900**

Just after 6 a.m. the North of Scotland Orkney & Shetland Steamship Company's mail steamer *St. Rognovald* ran hard aground in thick fog at Brough Head on the island of Stronsay, Orkney. Although the 70 or so passengers aboard were saved, a considerable amount of livestock aboard was lost and the general cargo and mail could not be saved either. A week after running aground, the ship slipped off the reef on which she had grounded and sank. Less than ten years before she had run aground in remarkably similar circumstances on the Head of Work, near Kirkwall.

STRUCK BY TWO SHIPS WITHIN TEN MINUTES, AND SUNK BY THE SECOND,
WITH THE LOSS OF OVER TWENTY LIVES: THE S.S. "ROWAN."

THE SHIP THAT CUT IN TWO AND SANK THE "ROWAN," ALREADY STRUCK
BY THE "WEST CHAMAK": THE "CLAN MALCOLM" AFTER THE COLLISION

BADLY DAMAGED BY RAMMING THE "ROWAN" AMIDSHIPS: THE BOWS
OF THE "CLAN MALCOLM," AFTER SHE WAS TOWED BACK TO GLASGOW.

SURVIVORS OF A PARTY OF 37, OF WHOM 19 WERE REPORTED SAVED: MEMBERS
OF THE SOUTHERN SYNCOPATED ORCHESTRA RESCUED FROM THE "ROWAN."

The Laird Line cross-Channel steamer "Rowan," outward bound from Glasgow to Dublin, collided with an American steamer, the "West Chamak," bound for Glasgow, at about 12.15 a.m. on October 9, in a fog off Corsewall Point, Wigtownshire. Suddenly, some ten minutes later, another ship (the "Clan Malcolm") loomed up and crashed into the "Rowan" amidships. The number

of missing was stated to be 28, out of 104 on board the "Rowan." H passengers included 37 members of the Southern Syncopated Orchestra, on th way to perform in Dublin. Nineteen were reported saved, including the co ductor, Mr. Egbert E. Thompson (second from right in our photograph), b one died after being rescued.—[Photographs by I.B. and C.N.]

26. Steamer *Rowan* sinks in collision, October 9 1921

The Laird Line S S *Rowan* sank on October 9 1921 whilst en route from Glasgow to Dublin with passengers. Off Corsewall Point on the Wigtownshire coast she was in collision with no less than two ships, the U S steamship *West Camak*, inward bound from San Francisco, and the Clan Line S S *Clan Malcolm*, en route from Glasgow to Liverpool. Around midnight the *Rowan* ran into dense fog and shortly after was struck from behind by the *West Camak*. Although damage did not appear to be serious at that stage, the Captain instructed that an SOS be sent and one of the nearest vessels was the *Clan Malcolm*.

As *The Scotsman* reported at the time: "A few minutes later the Clan Malcolm loomed up in the mist bearing directly upon the starboard of the Rowan. The passengers on the cross-Channel vessel were congratulating themselves on the promptitude with which assistance had arrived, when to their dismay the Clan Malcolm, instead of coming to a stand, crashed into the side of the vessel about midship with great violence." In less than a minute the *Rowan* had sunk and 34 passengers and crew, including her Captain, perished.

27. Swedish ship *Ustetind* aground Walls, Shetland, December 25 1929

This was the first motor vessel to be wrecked in Shetland. She was on voyage from Sweden to the Tyne with telegraph poles, dragged her anchor and went aground at Silwick, Walls, soon after getting into difficulty and losing a propellor. All of her crew of 11 were rescued by the Walls Rocket Brigade working in driving snow.

28. Swedish steamer *Borg* **aground Birsay Bay, Orkney, July 3 1931**
The *Borg* was en route from Leningrad to Belfast with a wood cargo when she struck the reef known locally as North Shoal, ten miles north of the Brough of Birsay. Luckily she contrived to beach at Birsay Bay and although she became a total loss most of her cargo was saved.

THE STORMS OF JANUARY & FEBRUARY 1953

29. Ferry *Princes Victoria* sinks, January 31 1953

The five-year-old, Clyde-built British Rail passenger and car ferry *Princess Victoria* set sail on her normal schedule between Stranraer and Larne at 7.45 a.m. on January 31 1953, in the midst of what became known as The Great Storm. Once out of the shelter of Loch Ryan she was almost immediately in difficulty and it is surmised that Captain Ferguson headed his vessel north, into the weather, prior to an attempt to return to Stranraer stern first. However, heavy seas smashed in her stern loading doors and she was forced to heave to in the weather. At 09.45 she radioed: "Hove to off mouth of Loch Ryan. Vessel not under command. Urgent assistance of tug required".
Drifting and taking in water on her car deck, she sent out a more urgent message at 10.31: "Four miles north west of Corsewall. Car deck flooded. Heavy list to starboard. Require immediate assistance. Ship not under command". The destroyer *Contest* set sail from Rothesay and at four minutes after eleven the Portpatrick lifeboat, *Jeanie Speirs*, left harbour. Unfortunately, there were no tugs available in the area. Equally unfortunately, those ashore were not advised by the casualty that the Captain had evidently decided to strike out for the shelter of the Irish coast and rescue vessels proceeded to the position off Corsewall Point in the Mull of Galloway. Before rescue ships eventually found her she capsized and sank with the loss of 133 lives more than 20 miles off course off the Irish coast at Donaghadee. Out of a crew of 49 and 125 passengers only 41 were saved; no women or children survived in the mountainous seas.

30. A crowded lifeboat from the *Princess Victoria* shelters in the lee of the tanker *Pass of Drumochter*. Conditions were too rough to take survivors aboard but the tanker sheltered the lifeboat until the Donaghadee Lifeboat and destroyer *Contest* arrived.

31. **Grounding of** *Clan MacQuarrie*
January 31 1953
Earlier in the day of the same Great
Storm which so disastrously sank
the ferry *Princess Victoria*, the
cargo vessel *Clan MacQuarrie* was
driven aground, whilst en route
from Hull to the Clyde, near the
village of Borve on the Isle of
Lewis. Under extremely difficult
conditions — the winds were
gusting to 100 mph — the
Stornoway Coast Lifesaving
Company travelled more than 20
miles to the wreck, manhandled its
equipment to the beach and
managed to fire a line to the ship.
In a little over two hours all 66
crewmen aboard were rescued in a
textbook operation. This
represented the largest number of
people ever rescued by breeches
buoy in a single operation.

32. **The Fraserburgh Lifeboat thrown up on the beach, February 9 1953**

33, 34. Arbroath Lifeboat, October 27 1953

Six crewmen were lost when the lifeboat *Robert Lindsay* capsized in Arbroath Harbour just before dawn. The lifeboat, commissioned in 1950, had joined the Anstruther Lifeboat in gales and heavy seas in an all night search after Elie Coastguard had reported seeing flares. Returning to station, she attempted to run before the seas into harbour but went over. There was just one survivor, local fisherman Archie Smith, who managed to grab a rocket line fired from the shore. "As I was floating away, I felt something strike my body and I made a grab at it in the water. It was a rope. I lashed it round my arm and was hauled in." It was widely surmised at the time that the distress flares had been fired by the Dundee sand ship *Islandmagee* which was lost that week with her crew of six on passage from Dundee to Leith.

35, 36, 37. **Fraserburgh Lifeboat (1919, 1953 & 1970)**

Disaster has overwhelmed the Fraserburgh lifeboat no less than three times this century. At the harbour entrance in April 1919 two members of the lifeboat crew were lost. At the same spot on February 9 1953 all but one member of the crew of seven of the *John and Charles Kennedy* drowned when she capsized in a heavy swell (see 32). From the beach hundreds of townsfolk saw the tragedy unfold but were unable to save their menfolk in the heavy breakers. The lifeboat had escorted several yawls to safety in the heavy seas which were running but one hour after its midday launch it was caught by a huge breaker and capsized, throwing the crew into the sea. Those ashore were powerless to assist and fishing vessels which went to the rescue could not get close enough into the beach.

A new lifeboat, *The Duchess of Kent*, was commissioned in 1953. Five members of the crew of *The Duchess of Kent* were lost on January 21 1970 when mountainous seas turned her over on her back 36 miles off Kinnaird Head as she escorted the Danish fishing boat *Opal* to safety (above). There was also one single survivor on this occasion: Jackson Buchan was picked up by a Russian trawler (above right) and the lifeboat was salvaged by a Russian fish factory ship. The lifeboat was of the non-self righting Watson type, the same as the Longhope boat lost with her crew of eight the previous year (q.v.). The wave which overturned the lifeboat was regarded as a freak wave and the accident was captured in this dramatic photograph. Below, the salvaged lifeboat in Buckie Harbour.

38, 39. Longhope Lifeboat capsizes, March 17 1969

Winds were gusting to hurricane force 11 in the North Sea on the night of March 17 1969. The Liberian registered ship *Irene*, on passage from Granton to Norway in ballast, was driven far off course and around nine that evening, running out of fuel, she was driven ashore on the Orkney island of South Ronaldsay at Grimness. In the foulest of weather conditions, with waves reportedly sixty feet high, both Kirkwall and Longhope lifeboats were launched. All radio contact with the Longhope lifeboat, *TGB*, a 47 foot non-self righting Watson type boat, was lost at 9.28 p.m. and although Wick Radio called her all night and a search by four other lifeboats was instituted it was not until the next day that the lifeboat was discovered capsized four miles west of Torr Ness, Hoy. The bodies of seven of the eight crew were found inside the lifeboat. The loss was a devastating disaster for the small community of Walls on the Island of Hoy which lost, in one cruel stroke, Coxswain Daniel Kirkpatrick, his two sons and five other men. Coxswain Kirkpatrick (left) had a particularly distinguished record in the lifeboat service, having won the RNLI Silver Medal for Gallantry no less than three times. The 17-man crew of the *Irene* were safely brought ashore by South Ronaldsay Rocket Brigade.

40, 41. The Storm of December 6/7 1959

While a search was going on for survivors from the Aberdeen trawler *George Robb* aground at Duncansby Head (all 12 crew were lost), Wick Radio received a distress call from the 360-ton Leith coaster *Servus*, bound for Wick when a shaft in the engine room broke. Buckie lifeboat went to her assistance, together with the fishery research vessels *Scotia* and *Explorer*, and the trawler *Aberdeen Progress*. The *Scotia* attempted an unsuccessful tow but a westward drift continued throughout the day, which suggested that eventually the coaster would run aground on the Caithness coast. The Buckie lifeboat was obliged to return to harbour for refuelling and the Wick lifeboat was unable to launch in the prevailing conditions. The Cromarty lifeboat put to sea and made contact with the crippled ship just one mile from the coast and disaster.

All eight of her crew were rescued before the *Servus* went aground and became a total loss. The galley boy was in no doubt about the lesson of his experience: "The *Servus* was my first ship and it will be my last. I don't intend to go back to sea again. I shall go back to my old job as a printer. This was a terrible ordeal and it has put me off sea-going completely".

As this drama was being enacted, another was just starting: the coastguard at Rattray Head sighted red flares from the Finnish cargo vessel *Anna* which was drifting off the coast on voyage from Riga to Leith. The engine room had become flooded, the pumps had failed and she was irretrievably drifting. Faced with the inevitability of her being driven ashore in the weather prevailing, the coastguard scrambled the Rattray and Fraserburgh LSA companies: the conditions were too severe to launch a lifeboat. She grounded at St Combs and in a long, difficult and hazardous operation all 18 of her crew were saved by breeches buoy (below). The ship became a total loss.

Early on the morning of December 7, the coastguard at Fife Ness observed that the North Carr light vesel had broken adrift from her moorings and called out the Broughty Ferry lifeboat, *Mona*, as well as lifesaving companies from Carnoustie and Crail. The Honorary Secretary of the Anstruther Lifeboat declined to launch, such were the conditions. Shortly before 5 a.m. the lifeboat radioed that she had cleared the bar at the entrance to the Firth of Tay and that she had sighted a red distress rocket form the drifting light vessel. That was the last message received from her. There was no further radio contact and such was the severity of the weather that no other flanking lifeboat stations could launch to investigate. Just before 9 a.m. Carnoustie coastguard sighted the missing lifeboat ashore at Buddon Ness on the north bank of the Tay (above) and the local lifesaving company found the bodies of seven of the crew in the cockpit and another body on the beach. The crew of the drifting light vessel were rescued by helicopter the next day.

42. HMS *Barcombe* aground off Mull

The boom defence vessel HMS *Barcombe* went aground January 13 1958 at Loch Buie in the south side of the Isle of Mull. There was initial confusion following a distress message at 9 o'clock that evening advising, "Believe I am aground Oronsay". For 17 hours the ship could not be traced by those searching for her. Lieutenant-Commander Derek Godfrey, who was in command of the ship, said: "The crew behaved well in adverse circumstances", after having sat on the side of the cliffs throughout the night and morning. They were eventually rescued by the Islay Lifeboat and the submarine tender *Kingfisher*.

43. Submarine *Narwahl* aground Trench Pt. Campbeltown

In May 1960 the submarine *Narwahl* ran aground at Trench Point near Campbeltown. Here naval salvage vessels attempt to pull her free.

44. Steamer *Lochiel* aground West Loch Tarbert

The 603-ton MacBrayne steamer *Lochiel* went hard aground in Escart Bay, West Loch Tarbert, in October 1960. A major salvage operation was launched and this photograph shows the steamer submerged at the bows, where she struck, with the salvage vessel *Plantagenet* lying alongside.

45. Aberdeen trawler *Craigievar* aground St Abbs Head
The Aberdeen pocket-size trawler *Craigievar* went aground on rocks at St Abbs Head at four on the morning of February 25 1960. After being pounded by seas for more than seven hours she was refloated and taken in tow. She struck the rocks less than 100 yards from where the Swiss ship *Nyon* (q.v.) had been wrecked the previous year.

46. Swiss cargo ship *Nyon* aground St Abbs Head
The 9,500 ton Swiss cargo ship *Nyon* was wrecked on rocks at St Abbs Head in November 1958. Despite a major slavage operation which involved three tugs, the St Abbs Lifeboat and fishing boats from Eyemouth, which landed tons of concrete to plug the holes made by the rocks, she remained hard aground.

47. Tug *Forager* **sinks in Clyde opposite Yarrows, May 24 1962**

Two men were trapped and drowned in the engine room of the tug *Forager* on May 23 1962 as she was escorting the 14,000 ton freighter *Hororata* upriver. The Steel & Bennie tug quite suddenly went down by the stern blocking the Clyde navigation channel opposite Yarrows' yard.

48. S S *Cliffville* **sinks at Meadowside Quay, Glasgow**

The 965 ton coaster S S *Cliffville*, complete with a 1,000 ton cargo of wheat, sank at her berth at Meadowside Quay, Glasgow, early on the morning of May 12 1958. One of her engineers discovered that she was taking in water and the crew scrambled ashore just before she sank. Firemen were unable to control the developing list and she settled on her side.

49. *Seaboard Intrepid* **aground Bressay, Shetland, July 7 1988**

This dramatic photograph shows the oil rig support vessel *Seaboard Intrepid* lodged firmly underneath the cliffs in Bressay Sound near the entrance to Lerwick Harbour.

TRAWLERS ASHORE

50. Polish trawler *Nurzec* **aground Balmedie, January 1974** (left)
Crew members of the Polish trawler *Nurzec* were rescued by helicopter and breeches buoy after the ship went aground at Balmedie, near Aberdeen.

51. Trawler *Summerside* **aground near Aberdeen, May 6 1970** (left, below)
There was a dramatic rescue by breeches buoy of the members of the crew of the Aberdeen trawler *Summerside* when she went aground on rocks to the south of Aberdeen.

52. Trawler *Navena* **aground Copinsay Rocks, Orkney, December 5 1973**
This dramatic aerial picture shows the the stricken Aberdeen trawler aground on a reef 300 yards offshore. Her crew of 12 were rescued from the afterdeck of the trawler in 100 m.p.h. winds by a British Airways helicopter.

53. Aberdeen trawler *Ben Barvas* **goes aground in the Pentland Firth, January 1964**
The Aberdeen trawler *Ben Barvas* ran hard aground on the Little Pentland Skerry on the night of January 3 1964. Although the trawler was to become a total loss, the crew of 14 were saved: five from a liferaft and the others, in an act of conspicuous bravery, were rescued by the Longhope Lifeboat (*q.v.*) under the command of Coxswain Daniel Kirkpatrick. The trawler was being washed by heavy seas, and the rescue was complicated by floating debris and diesel oil. The lifeboat got a line aboard and took nine crewmen off by breeches buoy under the most difficult of conditions. Here they are seen upon their return to Aberdeen with, *inset*, the launch of the *Ben Barvas*, June 1957.

54. Coastguard rescue helicopter sinks off Kinlochbervie, October 19 1989
The £ 2 million Sikorsky coastguard rescue helicopter based at Stornoway crashed
into 180 feet of water off Kinlochbervie whilst on a rescue mission. Her four man
crew managed to escape and on October 26 it was raised by the Peterhead based
salvage vessel *North Sea Commander.*

55, 56. Paddle steamer *Waverley*
aground on the Gantocks, near
Dunoon, July 15 1977
The P S *Waverley*, the last ocean
going paddle steamer in the world,
has enjoyed a colourful and at
times dramatic history. She has run
aground on several occasions and,
in this instance, went hard aground
on the Gantocks in the Clyde near
Dunoon. On the bridge is her
master, Captain David Neill.

57. Fishing vessel *Boy Andrew* sinks off Nizz Rock, Shetland, January 13 1989
This dramatic photograph shows the fishing vessel *Boy Andrew* sinking in heavy seas after being blown onto Nizz Rock, Shetland. Her crew were taken off by Lerwick Lifeboat, in the foreground.

58. *Piper Alpha* **explosion and fire, July 6 1988**

A massive explosion and huge fire engulfed the *Piper Alpha* oil
platform in the North Sea on the night of July 6 1988. There
were 229 men aboard and in this, the world's worst oilrig
disaster, 167 men died. The initial explosion was followed by
a fierce fire which, in turn, triggered off a further series of
explosions. There was no time to send a distress message and
the first news came shortly before 10 p.m. when the support
vessel lying off the rig, *Lowland Cavalier*, reported an explosion.
Many of those aboard had to jump hundreds of feet from the
platform into the sea — as one survivor graphically expressed
the horror of the situation, "It was jump and try or fry and die."

A massive rescue operation was launched. Civil and military
helicopters flying to the scene, from shore and from other rigs,
were able to see the flames from 25 miles away and, as they
came in at 200 feet, the flames towered above them. Early on,
an RAF helcopter from Lossiemouth could not approach nearer
than one mile because of the heat. An approaching Nimrod
aircraft from RAF Kinloss reported sighting flames 300 to 400
feet high from as far as 70 miles away. By coincidence, the
specialist oilfield firefighting vessel *Tharos* was on the scene
and although she directed all her pumps and jets onto the
platform she was quite unable to prevent its total destruction.
Standby vessels and other ships in the area of the rig made
many heroic rescue attempts but the fire was of such heat and
intensity that much of their effort was rendered futile. Many of
those who died were trapped in the accommodation module
and others perished as the helipad, where they awaited rescue,
was engulfed by fire. The first survivors, most suffering from
extensive burns, reached Aberdeen Royal Infirmary by
helicopter at 3.20 in the morning and as dawn broke over the
North Sea the full extent of the devastation became apparent.
Helipad, lifeboat stations and platform superstructure had been
blown into the sea and the derrick lay crazily twisted and
collapsed over the remains of the platform.

59. The day after the explosion and the rig continues to burn.

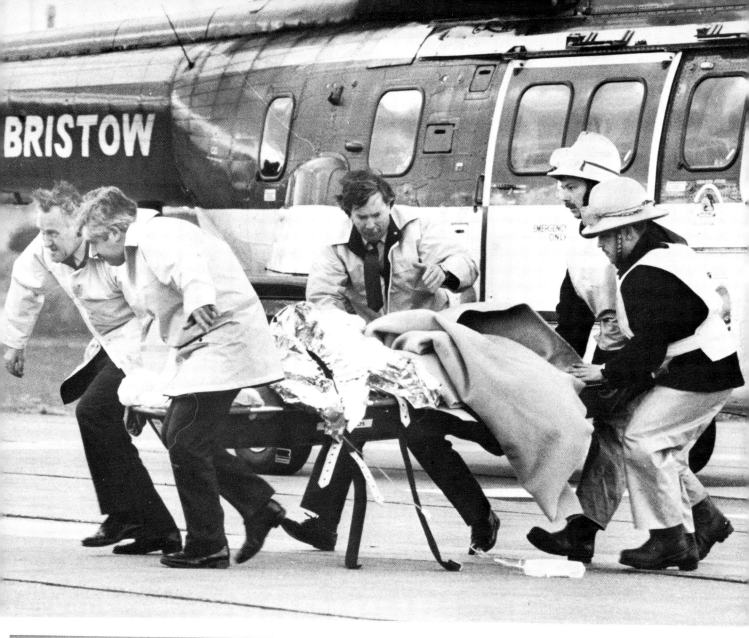

60. Survivors come ashore at the helipad at Aberdeen Royal Infirmary.

61. A massive international rescue operation was launched. Here a Dutch navy helicopter hovers above the platform.

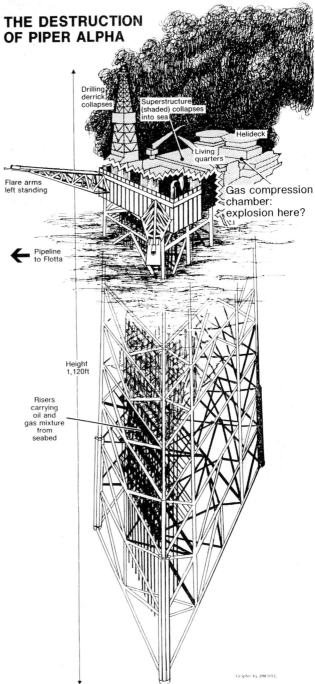

THE DESTRUCTION OF PIPER ALPHA

Drilling derrick collapses

Superstructure (shaded) collapses into sea

Helideck

Living quarters

Flare arms left standing

Gas compression chamber: explosion here?

← Pipeline to Flotta

Height 1,120ft

Risers carrying oil and gas mixture from seabed

Graphic by JIM HILL

62. A number of the wellheads continued to burn and it was not until July 20 that veteran Texan firefighter Red Adair put out the biggest fire on the still burning platform. As of Spring 1989 no cause for the explosion had been definitively identified and a longrunning official enquiry was still sitting in Aberdeen.

64. Dr Armand Hammer, President of Occidental Oil, owners of the platform arrives at Aberdeeen Royal Infirmary amidst massive media attention.

65. *Ocean Odyssey*, **explosion and fire, September 22 1988**
There was a narrow escape for 66 men on board the *Ocean Osyssey* drilling rig in the North Sea after an
explosion and fire, reminiscent of the July disaster on *Piper Alpha*. The radio operator stayed on the rig sending
distress messages and died in the fire. Here the damaged rig is seen berthing at Dundee.

NATURAL CAUSES

66. The army is brought in to sandbag the banks of the River Ness, Inverness floods, February 1989.

Severe weather is no stranger to the Scots. It most often manifests itself in loss of life at sea, although some storms wreak structural damage on land. The worst storms were arguably those of 1912, 1953, 1959 and 1968. The saving of life on land presents different problems from sea rescues and requires a quite different range of skills.

An increasing number of people choose to take to the hills at the weekends to enjoy the particular pleasures which the topography of Scotland offers. Most of these people are adequately equipped and, if not experienced themselves, take guides or colleagues acquainted with the dangers of mountain and hill. A minority persist in getting into difficulty and although calamities on the scale of the Cairngorm school party disaster are, fortunately, few and

far between, the rescue services have to be constantly on call. In the front line are the mountain rescue teams which, apart from the RAF one based at Kinloss, are made up of volunteers, much on the same basis as their counterparts in the larger lifeboat service. There are mountain rescue teams based in Lochaber, Glencoe, Fort William and the Tweed Valley: this last one played a major role in the Lockerbie disaster, locating and tagging bodies. In recent years they have been allocated new and improved communications facilities. This is the only area in which they are assisted from public funds, in this instance by the police. All the other equipment used is purchased by the members of the various teams.

An attempt has been made recently to combat the

avalanche menace by setting up an early warning system. It is doubtful whether the faithful search and rescue dog will ever be replaced as a means of locating the injured or dead below snow or ice, but new hand-held infra-red equipment is now in use, avalanche bleepers are carried in avalanche prone areas and experiments are currently being made into the efficacy of ground probing radar.

The rescue teams are backed up by a Sea King helicopter flight based at RAF Lossiemouth, the Bristow operated search and rescue helicopters at Stornoway and Sumburgh, Wessex helicopters at RAF Leuchars, Royal Navy Sea King helicopters at shorebased HMS *Gannet*, Prestwick, and, for long range use and maritime surveillance, Nimrod aircraft based at Kinloss. The nationwide Nimrod search and rescue role is shared between Kinloss and RAF St. Mawgan, in Cornwall. Dinghies, rations and flares are carried which, in case of need, can be dropped to parties in distress. All these units work under the command of the Northern Rescue Coordination Centre at RAF Pitreavie, near Edinburgh. They are all available to assist mountain rescue teams or, for that matter, any intensive search operation — such as that operated in the wake of the Lockerbie air crash.

Rain, wind and snow, in that they are frequent occurrences on an annual basis, are only noted when they are particularly severe; floods are always noted such is the havoc and inconvenience caused to those affected.

Modern communications have assisted in the mitigation of flood damage but no such aid was available in the Great Moray Flood of August 1829. In the first flood of that month, two days of heavy rain, combined with a wind from the north, turned the rivers into torrents. The Findhorn Bridge was swept away and there was, according to one contemporary account, "in all the plains of Morayshire but havoc and devastation . . . the Findhorn could no longer be called a river, and the whole of the rich and beautiful country was immersed, the wretched inhabitants were obliged to betake themselves to their house-tops . . . These ill-fated farmers and their families were carried off from their perilous positions by the Findhorn boats which came, full sail, over cornfields, bridges and dykes, to their relief."

In the second, much worse, flood a considerable number of stone bridges, including the Nairn Bridge already weakened in the first flood, were completely swept away and all that farmland not already destroyed in the first flood was quite ruined in the valleys of the Nairn, Findhorn, Lossie and Spey. Just how easily an apparently solid, well founded stone bridge can be carried away was demonstrated as recently as February 1989 when the railway bridge at Inverness was swept away.

Unlike most other causes of catastrophe, the weather is something over which man has very little, if any, control. Modern, sophisticated methods of forecasting have afforded a better chance of preparing against — and surviving — extreme conditions. Even then — as was the case with the great October gales in England in 1987 — the forecasters do not always get it right . . . .

Generally insanitary conditions, combined with limited medical prophylactic knowledge or facilities, brought epidemics of one sort or another to Victorian cities. By the early 1900s social reforms and improved knowledge were having a beneficial effect but terrible diseases were still visited upon the poorer classes especially. Scotland saw an outbreak of bubonic plague in 1900 which horrified observers at home and abroad: newspapers reported on August 28 that a child had sickened and died at a house in Thistle Street on the south side of the city. After other members of the family became ill it was confirmed that there was an outbreak of bubonic plague. Over the ensuing month more than 100 suspected cases were detained in Belvedere Hospital and six persons died.

In January and February 1907 there was widespread meningitis in Glasgow, Edinburgh and Belfast. In the month of January, 52 people died in Glasgow alone with over half the cases affecting children under five years. There was limited knowledge of the disease at the time and low temperatures were thought to be responsible. In Glasgow, the outbreak highlighted deficiencies in the management of the city's hospitals.

The First World War acted as something of a catalyst to medical knowledge and epidemics were soon to become — or so it was thought — something of the past. Thus the Aberdeen typhoid epidemic of 1964 was a very real shock to the community there and a reminder further afield that such outbreaks were latent below the surface of modern life.

67. Troon Flood, November 26 1912

A south-westerly gale of exceptional severity combined with heavy rain and high tides caused much flooding and chaos in the west of Scotland in November 1912. On November 26 ten people lost their lives in the storm and at Troon there was the most serious flooding in the history of the town. The water forced its way over the sea wall shortly before high tide and rushed "in considerable volume" down Portland Street and Ayr Street. As the wind increased in velocity all the streets in the vicinity of the Cross were rendered impassable by up to four feet of water. Shopkeepers had to shut their premises and people were marooned in their homes. Perhaps this postcard was one local trader's way of recovering his losses!

"The Troon Flood," 26th Nov., 1912.

PHOTO BY A. SHERRIFFS, M.P.S.
CHEMIST, TROON.

68. Floods of August 1948

There was widespread flooding in the south of Scotland during August 1948 following heavy rain. This is a postcard view of the floods in Eyemouth.

AFTER THE FLOOD, EYEMOUTH. 13.8.48.   C6053.

69. Powderhall Stadium, Edinburgh, August 13 1948
In the floods of 1948 Powderhall Stadium was under four feet of water.

70. Flooding in Edinburgh at Slateford Bridge, July 17 1953

71, 72. **Floods of August 1956**
Two views of the extensive flooding of August 1956: left, the
River Tyne overflowing at Haddington (August 28) and the River
Tweed at Peebles the same day.

73. **Maryculter floods, November 1951**
The unusual sight of a lifeboat to the rescue — inland! Here, Aberdeen Lifeboat, brought to the scene by road,
goes to the assistance of the douce Deeside residents of Maryculter.

74, 75, 76. Gales of January 15 1968

The hurricane force gales of January 1968 brought widespread destruction to the west of Scotland. There was extensive structural damage — particularly graphic is the picture (left) of the twisted wreckage of a huge crane in the dry dock at Greenock. Radnor Park Church in Clydebank was virtually destroyed and four people died in a tenement in Dumbarton Road, Glasgow, after the chimney head collapsed and crashed through the building. There is a gaping hole in the roof of another tenement in John Knox Street (left), where the same thing has happened. Twenty people were killed in the 100 m.p.h. gales.

77. Inverness railway bridge swept away, February 7 1989

Inverness's main railway bridge, carrying the only rail link between Inverness and the south, and the Highlands, suddenly collapsed without warning at 8.30 in the morning. Several days of heavy rain had turned the River Ness into a raging torrent of water and the bridge, built in 1862, had the entire central section swept away, leaving the rail track suspended in mid-air. Much of the rest of the bridge was swept away later in the day. Fortunately, this incident did not have the tragic consequences of the very similar Carrbridge accident of 1915 (q.v.): although a passenger train was due to cross the Inverness bridge just 90 minutes later.

CLEARING THE BUCHAN LINE NEAR ABERDEEN.

78, 79. Snow in north east Scotland, December 1908
There were severe falls of snow in north east Scotland in December 1908. Troops and the unemployed were called in to clear Union Street in Aberdeen which had become completely blocked, and several trains were buried on the Buchan line.

80, 81. Cairngorm school party tragedy, November 21 1971
Six Edinburgh schoolchildren and a teacher, all members of a montaineering club at Ainslie Park School, lost their lives on a weekend of sub-zero temperatures, strong winds and blizzards in the Cairngorm mountains. After failing to return to Lagganlia Hostel, Kincraig, a major search operation was mounted but only a young female instructor, Catherine Davidson, and one boy pupil, Raymond Leslie (seen opposite), survived from the party, which had set out from the top of the Cairngorm chairlift on one of the worst weekends of the winter to climb to Corrour Bothy. The leader of the Cairngorm montain rescue team and local police publicly condemned the attempt in terms of the distance and conditions involved.

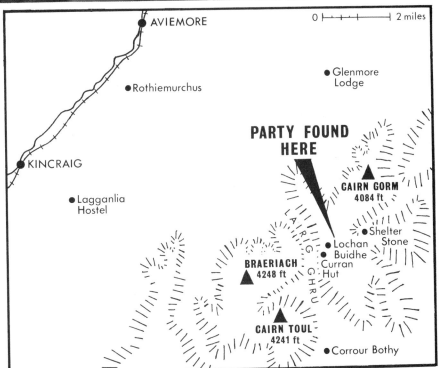

AVIEMORE

0 ⊢—┼—┼—┤ 2 miles

●Rothiemurchus

●Glenmore
Lodge

KINCRAIG

●Lagganlia
Hostel

**PARTY FOUND
HERE**

CAIRN GORM
4084 ft

●Shelter
Stone

●Lochan
●Buidhe
●Curran
Hut

BRAERIACH
4248 ft

CAIRN TOUL
4241 ft

●Corrour Bothy

82. Typhoid epidemic, Aberdeen, April-July 1964

In the early summer of 1964 an 11lb. can of corned beef from a city supermarket sparked off the typhoid outbreak. The spread was rapid and dramatic. The Medical Officer of Health for Aberdeen, Dr Ian MacQueen, became something of a celebrity as he faced the press and television daily throughout the crisis. By the end of April there were 136 reported cases and the city's schools had been closed.

83. Even the swings were closed !

84. This is the photograph which really said it all. Published all over the world and exhibited internationally, it epitomised the isolation which typhoid brought to Aberdeen.

FIRE

Total Destruction of Victoria Mills, Galashiels, June 26th, 1905.

Published by F. I. Walker, Bank Street, Galashiels.

85. Fire at Victoria Mills, Galashiels, June 26 1905
This locally published postcard — part photograph and part artist's embellishment
— depicts the spectacular blaze which totally destroyed Victoria Mills, Galashiels.

The worst urban conflagration in Scotland took place somewhat out of the time scale of this book — November 15—17 1824 — but the great fire which consumed the High Street, Parliament Square and the Tron Kirk in Edinburgh did very much affect what was to happen later in that it prompted improved techniques of fighting fire and caused insurance companies and property owners to look closely at the prevention of fires. As a contemporary commentator put it: ". . . the want of an experienced director, to regulate and give effect to the operations, was severely felt, and afterwards generally acknowledged". Between three and four hundred families lost their homes and those from all stations of life manned the pumps. Even the Lord Advocate "exerted himself with great activity and wrought for some time at the engines."

The most serious fires, especially in Central Scotland, have tended to be in out of date, often Victorian, unmodernised places of work. Fires like those at Cheapside and James Watt Street in Glasgow highlighted inadequate provision for fighting fires and, in the latter instance, a scant regard for worker safety. The Cheapside whisky bond fire involved the largest loss of life of firemen ever experienced in Britain — including the years of the blitz during the Second World War.

In 1987, 168 people died in fires in Scotland — almost half of them over the Christmas and New Year period. Domestic fires featuring loss of life have been — and still are — a persistent problem. The 'Saturday night booze and chip pan' syndrome is a rather more trite way of expressing what one 'senior fire brigade official' observed in January 1989, commenting upon a drop in fire deaths over the Christmas and New Year period related to the police crackdown on drinking and driving. "Normally, people would have arrived home well under the influence and acted the part of the galloping gourmet — cooking late night meals and falling asleep, leaving pans to go on fire. But this year, because of the anti-drink-driving campaigns, more people were arriving home sober, and therefore were less danger to themselves and others." That notwithstanding, 11 people died in fires in Scotland over the Christmas and New period, traditionally the worst time of the year for domestic fire deaths. The worst single house fire in Scotland was in Shettleston in August 1966 when a family of seven was wiped out.

The year 1978 brought its own particular pressures on the fighting of fires in Scotland. The firemens' strike put great pressure on the services fire crews and, inevitably, there was much loss of life and property which might not otherwise have taken place but for this bitter, long running dispute. The Grosvenor Hotel in Glasgow would probably not have been lost if the regular fire crews had been available.

Fires in public buildings are probably the most potentially hazardous in terms of loss of life but, fortunately, have not been frequent — a reflection of generally adequate precautions — with the only serious loss of life occurring at the Glasgow lodging house fire (1905), the Edinburgh Empire Theatre (1911) and Graftons' store in Glasgow (1949). In world terms these were but incidents compared to the Canton theatre fire (1845) which claimed 2,500 lives, the Vienna Ring Theatre fire (1881) which killed around 800 people or the L'Innovation department store fire in Brussels (1967) in which 322 shoppers died.

Modern firefighting equipment and techniques are today usually equal to the challenges presented by the worst of conflagrations given reasonably early notice and response time.

86. Glasgow lodging house blaze, November 19 1905

There were between three and four hundred occupants of the model lodging house in Watson Street, near Glasgow Cross, when fire broke out shortly before six in the morning. A converted warehouse, the building consisted of four floors, attic and basement which had been converted into dormitory accommodation for those of limited means. The bulding was lined with wood and the small cubicles constructed of timber. The fire started in one of the dormitories on the third floor: *The Scotsman* opined, "In all probability it was a spark from a morning pipe that caused the disaster." Although the fire brigade were on the scene within a few minutes of the alarm, the fire spread rapidly and many of those on the floor where the fire started were trapped. In all, 39 men died and 24 were injured. *The Scotsman* editorial the next day was critical of the operation of the establishment: "The absence of any proof of adequate foresight and preparation against a contingency of the kind within the building, the rapid spread of the fire by means of the wooden cubicles, and also the fact that means of escape or even of access to air from the uppermost storey was only obtained after a cripple's crutch had been used to break a way through the windows, more than hint at defects of arrangement and construction."

That same morning the cross channel steamer *Hilda* ran aground in fog and a snowstorm off St. Malo and of the 128 persons aboard only five were saved. That same editorial reflected it was "a curious illustration of the saying that misfortunes often run in couples".

opposite: A dramatic photograph of the blaze at the Cheapside whisky bond, March 28 1960.

87. Great Fire, Glasgow, August 17 1909

A postcard view of the aftermath of the great warehouse fire in the Ingram Street — High Street area of Glasgow which accasioned more than £ 250,000 worth of damage. Shops, offices and warehouses full of commercial goods were destroyed. The blaze originated in the premises of Messrs Harris & Dietrichsen, ladies' underclothing manufacturers, and spread rapidly through warehouses containing muslin, stationery and foodstuffs. Despite the efforts of 120 firemen, buildings in Ingram Street on a frontage of 240 feet were destroyed, 200 feet in College Street and 196 feet in Shuttle Street. The nearby Albion Halls were also destroyed.

90. Fire at the Empire Theatre, Edinburgh, 1911 (opposite)

The Empire Palace Theatre in Edinburgh, opened in 1892, was the most sumptuous of all in the renowned Moss Theatre chain, with its electric lighting and fine decoration. The theatre held an audience of 3,000 and the disaster which occured on the night of May 9 1911 might well have been even more serious. That evening the popular illusionist, the Great Lafayette, was appearing in one of his more dramatic adventures which featured a lion and a beautiful maiden. The scenario required the maiden to chose beween the harem of a sultan and being thrown to the lions and, having chosen the latter, the illusion consisted of the lion apparently leaping upon her. In fact, when the Great Lafayette, attired as a lion, sprang upon her a lamp on stage burst into flames and set the curtain alight; the fire spread to the scenery and was only prevented from affecting the auditorium by the prompt lowering of the safety curtain. As the audience left the theatre in orderly fashion, there was wholesale panic behind the scenes. The doors leading from the stage to the auditorium had been locked on the instructions of the secretive Lafayette and the emergency exits were blocked by scenery. In the ensuing conflagration he and nine members of his company were trapped on the stage and burned to death.

Great Fire, Glasgow, August 1909; Damage, £250,000

88. Mugdrum House, Fife, gutted by fire, January 1 1916

New Year's Eve of 1915 was a night of gales in Fife and when Mugdrum House near Newburgh caught fire the blaze rapidly spread, gutting the house completely. There was plainly little to be done — everyone was content to line up for a group photograph! This rare postcard view was produced locally as a real photograph and was, presumably, snapped up by all those in the picture.

89. Peebles Hydropathic blaze, July 7 1905

Shortly before eight o'clock on the evening of July 7, 1905 a fire started in the kitchen chimney at the Peebles Hydropathic Hotel, setting light to the upper floors of the kitchen block. The fire quickly spread to the main hotel building and, fanned by a westerly wind, within the hour the entire roof was ablaze. Thousands of people gathered to see the most spectacular blaze ever known in the Peebles area and by midnight the French renaissance style building was completely gutted. *The Scotsman* correspondent at the scene reported, "The spectacle of the burning mass on the hillside was such as will live long in their memories . . ." At the time, the lack of a motor fire engine in Edinburgh was commented upon after the Peebles brigade requested assistance. However, as a horse drawn appliance would have taken almost three hours to get to Peebles one was not sent.

PEEBLES HYDROPATHIC. JULY 1905.

91. Glen Cinema, Paisley, December 31 1929

One of the saddest disasters in Scotland of all time was the appalling catastrophe at the festively decorated Glen Cinema at Paisley Cross in Paisley on the afternoon of New Year's Eve, 1929 (1). Smoke from a smouldering Western cowboy film blew into the auditorium where a special childrens' matinee was being held and panic-stricken children stampeded for the exit. Seventy children aged between 5 and 14 were crushed, trampled or suffocated to death. The actual fire in the cinema was insignificant, being restricted to the film from the operating box, but such was the panic that was caused to the unsupervised children that all the victims died from asphyxiation and crushing. The fact that the door at the rear exit, to which many of the children made their way in efforts to escape, was barred also contributed to the scale of the tragedy (2). When it was eventually opened, rescuers were met by a six foot high heaped mass of children. Five families lost two or more children and one family lost three children and, as *The Scotsman* reported, "a pall of gloom overshadowed Paisley". This was the greatest disaster in the annals of the British cinema industry.

FIREMEN FIGHT DISASTROUS GLASGOW SHOP FIRE

on turntable ladders playing hoses through the windows of Grafton's store, in Argyle Street, Glasgow, while others ose over the roof on the right.   Thirteen persons lost their lives in one of the worst fires Glasgow has experienced for many years.

92. Fire at Grafton's Store, Glasgow, May 4 1949

Thirteen women and girls died in the fire which destroyed Grafton's four storey gown store in Argyle Street. The fire, discovered in a small room next to the lift shaft, spread with terrifying speed — an official of the firm said that the building was enveloped in just over a minute. Those on the top floors were forced to escape by clambering along the top storey ledge from a window, crossing the roof of the adjoining Argyle Cinema, and then dropping onto the roof of an adjoining building — where they were rescued by firemen with ladders. Some employees were forced to jump into Argyle Street where thousands of passers-by gathered at the spectacle. The *Evening Dispatch* reported: "So dense were the crowds that mounted police and military police had to assist in controlling them, and additional fire appliances and ambulances arriving at the scene were impeded by the throng." At the time, this was the most serious fire in Glasgow since the lodging house blaze of 1905 (q.v.).

13 DEAD IN GLASGOW FIRE

Girls Trapped as Flames Sweep Through Shop

FIREMEN battled for almost 90 minutes yesterday in the centre of Glasgow in efforts to release people trapped by a fire raging through the four-storey building occupied by Grafton's (Fashion Specialists) Ltd., in Argyle Street.

Thirteen died as a result of the blaze.   Nineteen were taken to hospital, one of them detained with serious injuries.

For long after firemen gained access to the building, the final death-roll was in doubt.

It was Glasgow's worst outbreak since, over 30 years ago, 20 people lost their lives in a fire in a model lodging house in Watson Street, near Glasgow Cross.

Five girl employees of the firm, assisted by two men, gained safety by climbing along a top storey ledge of the building, crossing the roof of the adjoining Argyle Cinema, and dropping a considerable distance to the corner of the roof of another clothing store, where escape ladders were brought up by firemen.

As the fire brigade were assembling escape mechanism in front of the building two girls either jumped or fell in their endeavours to climb down. One died of injuries while on the way to hospital.

Most of the bodies recovered were found together on one floor where girl employees had run seeking safety. They appeared to have died from asphyxiation.

TRAFFIC CONGESTION

Thousands of passers-by in Argyle Street watched the escape of employees from the top floor of the building So dense were the crowds that mounted police and military police had to assist in controlling them, and additional fire appliances and ambulances arriving at the scene were at first impeded by the throng Traffic congestion spread to neighbouring streets, with long lines of tram-cars and motor traffic held up, and for a period practically the whole of the through traffic of the city was affected by diversions.

Through traffic for tramcars in Argyle Street was resumed about four hours later.

A window-dresser raised the alarm when she opened the door of a small room beside the lift shaft and smoke poured out

Officials of the firm said the flames spread with lightning rapidity, and one of them estimated that the building was enveloped in just over a minute. About 80 girls, mostly administrative staff, were in the premises at the time. Several customers on the ground floor were got out safely immediately the alarm was raised.

'One of the firm's officials, who was in his office on the third floor, stated that when he ran downstairs the flames seemed to blow up suddenly. He got the customers out, and immediately instituted rescue efforts for the staff employees on the top flat.

An employee, who sustained burning injuries, explained that he was on the bottom floor when the fire broke out. He immediately made his way to the upper flats, and was able to help several people to make their escape. By this time the building was like an inferno, and in his rescue work he sustained severe burns to his right hand. His hair and eyebrows were scorched. He was able to make his way to a stair at the back of the building, and from there was taken by ambulance to hospital, where he received attention.

Jean Gordon, a 17-year-old employee, who lives at 60 Royston Hill, told of her own escape. "Some of us managed to climb through a window on to the roof," she said. "We were glad to see a ladder stretching down to the street."

RAPID SPREAD OF FLAMES

A girl employee in a footwear shop opposite also described how swiftly the fire caught hold. She heard screams, and at first could see nothing. Then smoke began to issue at different points, and the building was rapidly enveloped.

Constable Hector Campbell, who was on

points duty at Argyle Street and Mille Street, send an alarm for the fire brigade when he saw smoke issuing from two third floor windows. He said that although at first there were only two puffs of smoke within a short time dense black smoke was belching out.

With some danger of the flames spreading to adjoining buildings, the audience of over 100 in the Argyle Cinema were evacuated as a precautionary measure, though the building remained undamaged.

Stocks were also removed hastily by employees of neighbouring clothing stores, who could be seen working feverishly on their task with wet handkerchiefs tied over their mouths to protect them from the choking smoke.

Shoppers in nearby premises found themselves locked away from entrances fronting Argyle Street in the immediate vicinity of the fire, and they had to leave from side exits.

The work of the firemen fighting the blaze was made difficult by the dense clouds of black smoke.

While some of the firemen poured water into the front of the building from fire towers other men worked from the rear to effect an entrance as soon as the intense heat and suffocating smoke would permit.

There was another alarm some four hours later, when it was discovered that adjoining premises, another gown shop, had caught alight. The outbreak was slight, and was quickly brought under control. The intense heat from the blaze in the building occupied by Grafton's had, according to a fire official, travelled through to the other shop, and had caused the second outbreak. A fire engine standing on the opposite side of the street was quickly wheeled into position, a line of hose was run out, and the flames were soon subdued.

94. William Mutrie's ablaze at Bells Brae, Edinburgh, May 9 1957

This spectacular blaze in Edinburgh's Dean Village destroyed the 200 year-old, three storey premises of theatrical costumiers William Mutrie & Sons, at the time the largest business in Britain dealing in theatrical costumes and scenery. In the blaze, 90,000 costumes were destroyed, as was the complete set and costumes for the West End production of *The King and I*.

93, 95. The fires at C & A Modes and C W Carr Aitkman, Edinburgh

Probably the two most spectacular blazes in Edinburgh in the 1950s took place within 24 hours of each other. On the night of November 10 1955 the C W Carr Atkman warehouse in Jeffrey Street was completely destoyed by fire (*right*) and, the next day, the C & A Modes department store in Princes Street was severely damaged by a fire which necessitated its complete rebuilding.

96. The scene at Carr Aitkman's warehouse the morning after the blaze.

97, 98. Gaumont Cinema, Edinburgh, May 31 1962
Firemen fight the fierce fire at the Gaumont Cinema, Edinburgh; water is poured onto the burning roof by a fireman perched on a turntable ladder.
The devastated interior of the Gaumont the next day (below).

99. Tranent Primary School on fire, February 12 1958

100. Rutherglen tenement blaze, May 12 1962
Four people died when fire broke out at this Rutherglen
tenement in 1962.

101. Barrowland Ballroom, August 20 1958
The scene after Glasgow's famous Barrowland Ballroom was
gutted by fire in 1958.

102. Aberdeen Grammar School, July 1 1986
Aberdeen Grammar School was gutted by fire in July 1986 after
a decorator set fire to a window frame whilst it was being
stripped. The impressive granite building was quickly reduced
to a shell in the spectacular blaze which followed.

103. Whisky warehouse fire Glasgow docks, March 20 1960
This was the first — and less serious — Glasgow whisky
warehouse blaze of March 1960. The consequences of the
following week's fire at Cheapside were not simply limited to
the loss of stocks of whisky. Here firemen salvage whisky.

104. Glasgow whisky bond fire, March 28 1960

Nineteen firemen died just after seven in the evening fighting the fire at the Cheapside whisky bond. Within five minutes of tackling the fire, the walls blew out unexpectedly with enormous force, striking the walls of the buildings opposite and then collapsing into the street below. Firemen, and three fire appliances, fighting the fire in Cheapside Street were buried in masonry from both sides. The fire, which spread to a tobacco warehouse next door, an ice cream factory and Harland & Wolff's engine works, took a week to extinguish completely, fed by a great lake of thousands of gallons of whisky in the basement. At the time this was Glasgow's worst blaze since the lodging house fire of 1905. Four million pounds worth of whisky and tobacco was destroyed. There was criticism at the time of the siting of the whisky bond and certainly the narrowness of Cheapside Street and Warrock Street had contributed significantly to the danger to firefighters.

105. Scene at the funeral of the firemen who died fighting the blaze.

108. Abeerdeen Combworks, April 1969
One of Aberdeen's most spectacular blazes destroyed the city's combworks. This dramatic photograph was taken from the top floor of the nearby Gallowgate flats.

107. James Watt Street fire, November 18 1968
Twenty-two workers died behind the barred windows of a three storey warehouse in Glasgow's James Watt Street which housed an upholstery business: the building had previously been used as a bonded warehouse. Steel bars over all the windows prevented all those inside except three from escaping and bodies were found piled behind a padlocked fire exit; others died in a lift trapped between floors and the complete destruction of the building's wooden straircases also impeded escape. One of the survivors described how the showroom "went up like a box of fireworks". Eye witnesses described the tragic and futile attempts of those trapped in the building: "We could see faces behind the first-floor windows but they had no chance of forcing the iron grilles barring their escape." Despite the attentions of 20 fire units, the building was reduced to a burnt out shell.

109, 110, 111. **Grosvenor Hotel blaze, Glasgow, January 7 1978**

In the ninth week of the 1978 firemens' strike Glasgow's 100-bedroom Grosvenor Hotel was destroyed in a spectacular blaze which raged out of control for six hours. The fire began just after 8 p.m. in the kitchen of the steakhouse of the luxury Reo Stakis hotel and despite the attentions of 60 Servicemen manning ten 'Green Goddess' fire engines taken out of mothballs for the duration of the strike, lack of proper firefighting appliances, such as turntable ladders, meant that they were quite unable to bring the blaze quickly under control. Instead the firefighters concentrated on preventing the blaze spreading to residential property further along the terrace. The hotel was a total loss. It was, however, completely rebuilt by its owner, Mr Reo Stakis pictured below, faithful to its original A-listed Venetian style

Earlier that day, Royal Navy firefighting teams fought a fire in which three members of the same family died at Linwood, Renfrewshire.

112, 113. Inverary Castle, November 5 1975

Inverary Castle, one of Britain's finest examples of an 18th century castle built in the French style and crammed full of antiques and art treasures, was seriously damaged by fire in 1975: as can be seen from this photograph, taken the morning after the fire, the castle roof and top floor were almost completely destroyed in the six hour blaze. Fortunately, most of the treasures were rescued intact by estate workers, local firemen from Dunoon and Glasgow Salvage Corps. Paintings and books were carried outside and then heaped onto lorries and into cars and taken to the village hall. After a successful appeal campaign the Castle was restored to its former glory. This was the third fire in the Castle's history. In 1877, the central tower was destroyed by fire and in 1950 roofing and a staircase at the eastern end of the building were destroyed.

ROAD, RAIL & AIR

BARASSIE DISASTER.

114. Barassie rail disaster, February 4 1898
Seven people were killed on the Glasgow & South Western Railway at Barassie near Troon when the Ayr—Glasgow 'boat' goods train and Kilmarnock—Ayr mail train collided.

The modern age of transport accidents was ushered in as long ago as 1830 at the Grand Opening of the Liverpool & Manchester Railway: the unfortunate victim, Mr Huskisson, oblivious to new fangled dangers, crossed the line to speak to the Duke of Wellington and was promptly run down by Stephenson's famous *Rocket*. The causes of railway accidents are, in numerical terms, few and in those early days inadequate brake power was a major culprit.

Scotland's first major railway disaster was indeed spectacular. On the night of Sunday, December 28, 1879, Sir Thomas Bouch's new railway bridge across the Tay collapsed taking with it, into the stormlashed waters 160 feet below, an engine, six coaches and 75 passengers. Elementary faults in the design and construction of the bridge were to blame.

The number of causes of railway accidents are limited by the working of the system and they are today comparatively rare compared to the situation in the 19th and early 20th centuries. In the old days, single track working contributed to many accidents but in more recent times the causes tend to boil down to signalling failure, excessive speed, obstructions on the line or the fallibility of railway employees. Human error of one sort or another has been at the root of many railway accidents over the last century. The worst railway disaster in Britain at Quintinshill Junction, Gretna, was caused entirely by human negligence and, indeed, resulted in prison sentences for two signalmen.

Terrorism, and the associated risk of sabotage, have become seemingly inextricably linked with travel in recent times. These are factors which had not featured notably in Scotland until the 1988 Lockerbie disaster, the only previous incidents centring around the activities of the IRA and the Scottish Republican Army.

Towards the end of October 1931 there was a rash of farm fires in the Dundee area followed by three potentially more serious attempts at sabotage. During the last week of October, two slow moving goods trains struck rails deliberately placed across the line and, on the night of October 30, a length of rail weighing 2 cwt. was placed across the main Aberdeen line at Broughty Ferry. Only by sheer chance did the main Aberdeen to London express passenger train not come to grief. Fortunately, these activities were unsuccessful and, according to John Baker White who was carrying out a private investigation into the wrecking campaign, they were carried out "by the Irish Republican Army in preparation for a more intensive and much more damaging campaign which never took place, partly because of the split in the higher command of the IRA that took place in June 1932, and because of the counter measures of the Ulster CID and our own Special Branch." According to Baker White, there was an organised company of the IRA at that time based in Leith.

The Scottish Republican Army raised its head in the 1950s. On the night of January 4 1956, a small bomb was thrown into the headquarters of the Territorial Army in Edinburgh but caused little damage. There were other isolated instances of the bombing of letterboxes.

The Lockerbie attack was on a quite different scale. The tranquil Borders town of Lockerbie is as about as far removed from the world of international terrorism as one could possibly imagine but, within a matter of hours of the disaster taking place, terrorism was being mooted as the cause by media-appointed experts. What was clear at that stage — and little more — was that an incident of extraordinary violence had taken place at 31,000 feet which had occasioned loss of power and structural breakup of the 747 aircraft. Basically, there were only three likely causes of such a sudden catastrophe: mid-air collision, a terrorist bomb or massive structural failure resulting in decompression and the grounding of the plane. Air traffic control information eliminated the first possibility at an early stage which left only the possibilities of a bomb or structural failure.

At that stage both possibilities promised further serious implications. If the bomb theory were to be proved then the attack on the Pan Am jumbo and the loss of so many American lives would prompt an immediate investigation into which group was responsible and, in all likelihood, retaliatory action of a military nature. If, on the other hand, a massive structural failure were to be found then the financial implications for Pan American Airways, already in deep financial trouble after having been bailed out by the US government, would, in all likelihood, turn out to be fatal. Added to which, the Boeing company and all airlines flying the 747 — then making around 700 flights every day throughout the world — would all find themselves in a quite disastrous situation. So, much was riding on the findings of the crash investigators who, in those early days, were extremely careful not to jump to the conclusions many others were coming to.

Bafflingly, there was no convincing claim of responsibility by any terrorist group although there was widespread speculation that the bomb was planted by a Middle East terrorist group, possibly in retaliation for the shooting down of an Iranian airliner with the loss of 290 lives by United States forces in the Gulf in July 1988.

Following the confirmation of terrorist attack, it was stated by Dr Bruce Hoffman, an expert on international terrorism at the Los Angeles-based Rand Corporation, that only 39% of such crimes are ever claimed by their perpetrators. Evidence was certainly produced of an anonymous threatening telephone call made to the US Embassy in Helsinki advising of a violent attack on a Pan Am plane, but this was only one advice amongst many dozens apparently regularly received every single month and it was later discounted by the Finnish police. So, terrorism was not the incontrovertible option it might have appeared at first sight.

It also has to be borne in mind that, despite all the apparent sophistication of modern scientific investigation techniques, it can still be very difficult to establish quickly the cause of such an in flight accident. It was never definitively proved what caused the 1985 downing of Air India flight 182, a Boeing 747 which crashed into the Atlantic west of Ireland. Admittedly, the investigation was rendered even more difficult than usual by the fact that wreckage had to be recovered from the seabed over a six mile radius, but, nevertheless, a remarkably detailed picture was built up from maps and salvage operations. As at Lockerbie, the cockpit voice recorder tapes were inconclusive with the same unidentifiable noise before recording ceased, presumably as a result of loss of power.

The circumstantial indications were that a bomb had been responsible after investigations by the RCMP in Canada and the disaster is generally regarded as having been caused by terrorist agency. There was, however, no definitive evidence of this from examination of bodies and wreckage.

Similarly, the Comet crashes of January and April 1954, in which airliners were completely destroyed off Elba and the Straits of Messina respectively, seemed to bear all the marks of sabotage: both had blown up within minutes of leaving the same airport, Rome, and neither sent out a Mayday before exploding at maximum altitude on full power. In both cases, the explosion appeared to be particularly violent. And, as prior to Lockerbie, there were stories of mysterious persons observed at Rome airport prior to the accidents. Only after an intensive enquiry was it established that, in fact, the accidents were both due to structural failure.

The explanation of the fate of Japan Air Lines Boeing 747 flight 123 was more clear cut. That aircraft took off from Tokyo's Haneda Airport on August 12 1985 and was in serious trouble within twelve minutes of take off. A loud bang from the rear of the plane brought the unwelcome news that a section of the aft fuselage had fractured and the cabin quickly depressurised. This was an example of the third possible scenario, which Lockerbie investigators had to bear in mind. Although Flight 123's flying controls and hydraulic systems were lost the pilots did manage to exercise some sort of control over the crippled airplane for more than thirty minutes and were in radio contact with the tower for this period. But after 32 minutes the aircraft crashed at a height of 4,780 feet into the side of Mount Osutaka, 70 miles north west of Tokyo.

The wreckage of Pan Am 103 indicated that a catastrophic failure had occurrred at the rear of the cockpit section, immediately severing power and control, hence the failure of radio communications, power and voice recorder. The cockpit itself crashed to earth remarkably complete, together with crew members strapped inside, having clearly parted company with the rest of the plane, which tumbled to earth disintegrating as it neared the earth. According to eye witnesses who saw it at an earlier stage in its descent, it was *not* on fire initially and it seems that it was only as it neared the impact point that major fire broke out. The lack of lighting aboard, noted by eye witnesses, suggests the total loss of power which would have been caused by the splitting off of cockpit section at the time of structural failure or explosion.

On December 28, Mick Charles, the chief investigator for the Air Accident Investigation Branch of the Department of Transport, announced at a press conference in Lockerbie that there was "conclusive evidence" of a high explosive detonation. Following examination of wreckage at the Royal Armament Research and Development Establishment at Fort Halstead in Kent, he stated unequivocally that "the explosive's residues recovered from the debris have been positively identified and are consistent with the use of a high performance plastic explosive . . . two parts of the metal luggage pallet's framework show conclusive evidence of a detonating high explosive." The preliminary conclusion was that the detonation took place at 31,000 feet shortly after the aircraft crossed the Scottish border. The Chief Constable of Dumfries & Galloway had reluctantly acquired the most massive international investigation his Constabulary had ever had on its hands. The Lord Advocate soon confirmed that jurisidiction applied in Dumfries and Galloway as the actual crime had taken place in the skies above and had brought about loss of life in the area, but he did point out that as an American registered airplane was involved any miscreants apprehended could be tried in any country party to international conventions governing air travel . . .

That notwithstanding, it would have been naive for any of those involved to rate very highly the likelihood of bring international terrorists to book — in the Sheriff courthouse at Dumfries, or anywhere else for that matter. Although newspaper reports over the following months were to report unprecedented international cooperation from sources as widespread and diverse as Yasser Arafat and the PLO, the Czech manufacturers of Semtex, the FBI and CIA in Washington, West German intelligence and their Israeli counterparts, Mossad, it was also clear that the most important answers in the dragnet would probably lie in virtually impenetrable centres of intrigue like Beirut, Damascus, Tripoli and Teheran. The rival and conflicting interests of different intelligence services also brought a political dimension to the problem — effectively removing it from the area of any normal police investigation. It has been widely suggested that the police officers in charge of the investigation, headed by Chief Superintendent John Orr of Strathclyde Police, would only hear carefully filtered information handed down by more powerful political and intelligence sources, although Scotland's Lord Advocate Peter Fraser (who succeeded Lord Cameron of Lochbroom in January 1989) was to angrily attack what he regarded as misleading and purely speculative newspaper reports.

The most important breakthroughs in the coming months were to be made by the forensic scientists and specialist crash investigators who were to literally piece together the shattered jumbo and its contents. This painstaking work enabled the investigators to establish by the middle of February 1989 that the explosive device which destroyed the aircraft had been placed within a radio cassette recorder and this was announced at a press conference held in Lockerbie on February 16. This information, it was little realised, had, however, been leaked a week previously by the *Jerusalem Post*, presumably tipped off by Mossad, and the report was repeated in the *Sunday Telegraph* of February 12.

In fact, security staff at Heathrow and other international airports had been on the lookout for radio cassette recorders holding bombs since November 22, a full month before Lockerbie. This alert arose directly out of a raid by West German anti-terrorist police on October 27 on a small flat in the Sandweg, Frankfurt. Inside the flat occupied by Palestinians, in an unremarkable street near to the zoo and heavily populated by students, police found a Japanese made radio cassette recorder, ironically brand named the Toshiba Bomb Beat 453, and which had been converted into a bomb. There were two activating devices: the first a timer, which would, in turn, activate the second, a barometric device which could be set to detonate explosives, such as Semtex, once the aircraft reached a predetermined height — say its cruising altitude of 30,000 feet. Alternatively, such a device could be used as the

115. Inchgreen rail accident, July 11 1906
On the line from Princes Pier, Greenock, to Overton Paper Mill in Ayrshire, a runaway train jumped the embankment at the foot of a hill and landed in a field. The driver was killed and the brakesman was charged with culpable homicide, but was acquitted on a majority verdict.

primer for a considerably larger charge of Semtex moulded, say, into the lining of the suitcase in which the radio cassette recorder was contained.

The aircraft baggage container carrying the bag which contained the bomb was meticulously reconstructed by scientists using parts recovered from 32 sites over an 800 square mile area stretching from Lockerbie itself to the Kielder Forest in Northumberland. The reconstruction work indicated that the the bag containing the bomb was loaded onto the container at Frankfurt airport. More than 10,000 pieces of personal property were also recovered and examined inside a disused factory at Lockerbie while pieces of the aircraft itself — representing 80% of the structure — were collated and reassembled in grids on the concrete floor of a five acre empty warehouse at the Ministry of Defence armaments depot, 20 miles away at Longtown.

The progress made by the investigation over the first ten weeks effectively vindicated the decision to run it from the crash area in the Scottish borders. The work of the forensic experts was probably best carried out as near to the locus as possible, and up to date computer techniques were employed to facilitate not only the collation of information but its instant communication to other interested parties. What everybody accepted, however, whether or not they would publicly admit it, was that investigation of one of the crimes of the century had effectively landed on the unwilling hands of police officers with, hardly unexpectedly, little experience of such a wide ranging enquiry with international and political ramifications. Dumfries and Galloway police were, in fact, handling the largest multiple murder investigation ever conducted in the United Kingdom.

Daily Record

THURS
JAN 29
1959

2½ᵖ SCOTLAND'S NATIONAL NEWSPAPER
No. 19,733

HERO DIES IN TRAM INFERNO

HOW IT HAPPENED

A SHEET of flame, sparked by 600 volts of electricity, set a tram ablaze seconds after it crashed into a lorry yesterday.

And in four minutes, the freak, 1000-to-1 accident killed three people.

The horror happened in the fog in Old Shettleston Road Glasgow. The people who died were the tram-driver and two women.

Freak accident

And last night, Glasgow's Firemaster Martin Chadwick said:

"It was a freak accident the point of impact was right on the tram's most vulnerable point . . .

". . the electric resistance control gear panel, an area about 2 ft. by 6 ft. on one end of the tram.

"It is situated just behind the driver's seat. And in this case the driver was sitting there.

"The impact caused the shearing of wires which started arc-ing.

"This is the flash which jumps between two unpro-tected electric wires.

No doubt

"There is no doubt about what caused the fire. It was this 600-volt charge. It would be powerful enough to set fire to almost anything."

Firemaster Chadwick went on: "An accident like this could happen any time. It could even happen to a fire engine.

"But it was a chance in thousands.

"There is no reason why the trams cannot run as they nor-mally do. You cannot take into account circumstances like this."

An inquiry

Mr E. R. L. Fitzpayne, the city's transport boss, said:

"I have been given no tech-nical reason to suppose that there is any abnormal danger in continuing the service as usual tomorrow."

An inquiry under the direction of the Transport Ministry will begin this morning.

NO NEW TRAMS are being built for Glasgow. By the end of 1961 only the present 250 Coronation streamlined trams will be in operation.

By 1963 the ity plans to abolish trams and complete the switchover to trolley buses and buses.

● WEAK POINT IN A TRAM'S ARMOUR and

● DEAD HERO WAS TO HAVE WED TODAY—Page 3

● FULL STORY — Centre Pages

● WHAT THE RECORD SAYS—Page 2

① At the very instant that this picture was taken, people were struggling for life... dark shapes which can be seen on the upper deck are passengers who eventually leapt to safety—most of them injured. Near the far end of the tram (as seen in this dramatic picture) died the driver.

MORE PICTURES on CENTRE PAGES

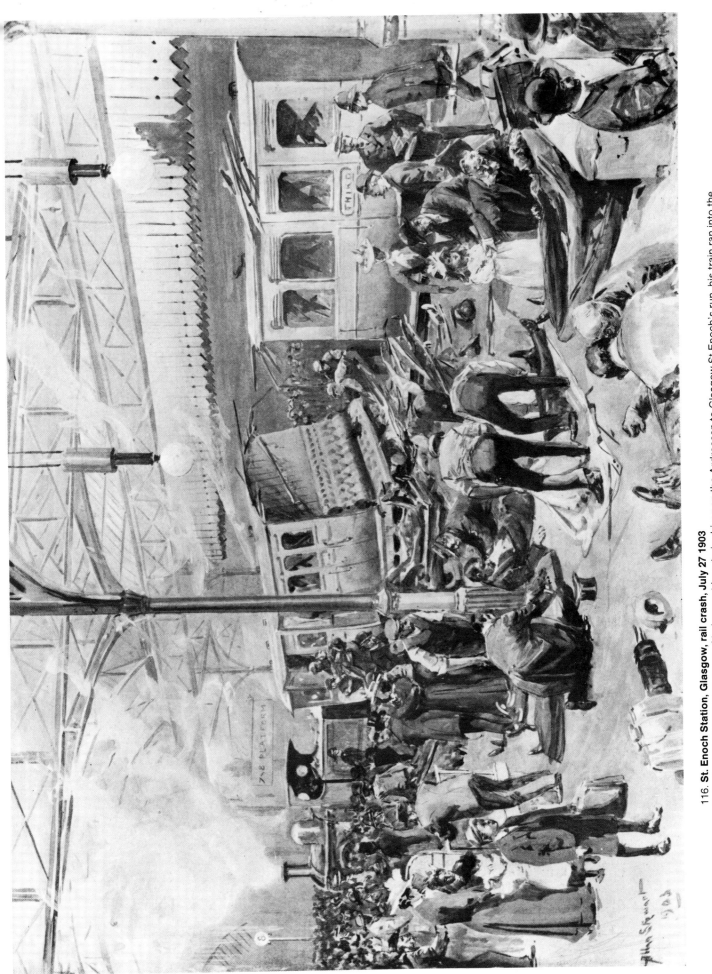

116. **St. Enoch Station, Glasgow, rail crash, July 27 1903**
Entirely as the result of an error of judgement by a train driver on the Ardrossan to Glasgow St Enoch's run, his train ran into the buffers at 10 m.p.h., despite the application of the brakes. The first and second carriages telescoped and 16 passengers were killed.

THE ELLIOT JUNCTION RAILWAY DISASTER, NEAR ARBROATH. DEC 28 1906

117. Elliott Junction railway disaster, Arbroath, December 28 1906

Curiously, this accident, also partly the result of extreme weather, happened on the 27th anniversary of the Tay Bridge disaster. In severe weather, the express from Edinburgh was forced to terminate at Arbroath as the line was blocked ahead. Meantime, a goods train heading south ran into a snowdrift and broke into three sections. Attempts to reconnect were abortive and some of the wagons became derailed. In consequence, a local train had to be held up. As single line working was introduced, snow brought down the telegraph lines. Scenes of great confusion followed and in driving snow the Edinburgh express set off back up the line to Dundee, tender first as it had proved impossible to use the turntable. At Elliott Junction the southbound train ran into the back of a stationary local train at an estimated 30 m.p.h. The three back coaches were totally destroyed; the engine of the express mounted the wreckage and overturned. A total of 21 passengers and the fireman of the express died. It later transpired that snow on the signal had made it appear 'clear' as it drooped under the weight. The driver of the express was considered to be proceeding too fast and admitted that he had accepted "something to keep the cold out" at Arbroath Station. Matters were made worse by the fact there was no equipment for dealing with an accident and it was not until next day that a breakdown train arrived. Both the weather and railway organisation contributed to this unfortunate accident.

THE OVERTURNED ENGINE.
Fife Railway Disaster, 14th April 1914.

Albany Serie

118. The Fife Railway Disaster, April 14 1914 (opposite)

Early on the morning of April 14 1914 the Edinburgh to Aberdeen express collided with the engine of the Carlisle to Dundee goods train at Burntisland Station. The northbound train was completely wrecked and the driver and fireman were both killed; twelve passengers were injured. The 120 ton engine, pictured here, left the railway line and leapt clear of the railway bed onto Burntisland Links where it plunged into the sands. One of the passengers, Mr Robert McLenann of McLennan & Co., bakers of Fraserburgh, ascribed the cause of the accident to the goods train being on the same line as the northbound express. Although it was at the time being backed into a siding to leave clear passage, there had evidently been a fatal miscalculation of the distances involved and in consequence the express had hit the other train at approximately 30 m.p.h.

Burning train, Gretna Green Railway Disaster May 22, 1915.

119, 120. Gretna rail disaster, May 22 1915

Three trains were involved in the horrific Gretna rail disaster at Quintinshill Junction: a special troop train, bearing the Seventh Royal Scots from their depot at Leith, Edinburgh, to Liverpool for embarkation to France, ploughed into the standing local train from Carlisle and this wreckage was then struck by the night express from Euston. The signalmen at Quintinshill, intent upon writing up their paperwork, had quite simply forgotten about the 'local' standing outside their signal box, which should have been shunted into the local loop line, and had given the troop train a clear signal. The impact was enormous: the 'local' had its brakes applied and the troop train telescoped to almost half of its normal length. The signalman had also accepted the express from the south and it ploughed into the debris and a loco tender blocking its route. This is the worst railway accident in British history with a death toll of 227. The two signalmen were blamed and subsequently served terms of imprisonment.

Attending the wounded. Gretna Green Railway Disaster, May 22nd, 1915

121. Carrbridge accident, June 15 1914

This was truly one of those unpredictable accidents. After a cloudburst above Carrbridge the burns coming down from the Grampians turned to spate and an old stone roadbridge above the railway was destroyed, the debris forming a dam. As the 10 a.m. train from Glasgow to Inverness pulled out of Carrbridge station the dam broke and a torrent of water, trees and boulders assailed the reilway bridge beyond the station as the train of six coaches passed over it. The train ground to a halt as the engine cleared the bridge and the front two coaches derailed, but three coaches still stood upon it. The fourth coach fell into the flood although, fortuitously, couplings held and the others remained on the bridge. Five passengers died.

122. Birmingham/Glasgow express fire, Beattock Summit, June 8 1950

Five people lost their lives when fire broke out on the Birmingham —Glasgow express near Beattock Summit. The three leading coaches were involved, the second and third of which were completely burnt out in the fire which started just before five in the afternoon. The affected coaches were uncoupled from the train but when firemen arrived they described the blaze as "like a furnace".

123. Glasgow/Edinbugh line crash at Castlecary, December 10 1937
Disaster followed when points became blocked by snow on the Edinburgh—Glasgow line berween Castlecary and Gartshore. The express train from Edinburgh was travelling at more than 60 m.p.h. when it hit the rear of a stationary express from Dundee pushing it a full 50 yards forward down the track. Thirty-five passengers were killed and 179 injured. A degree of blame was attached to the signalman at Castlecary whose procedure left much to be desired. Questions also were raised about allowing express trains to maintain such high speeds in visibility seriously reduced by falling snow.

124. The Edinburgh to Glasgow train crashed at Polmont, February 1962

125. Disaster at Paisley Gilmour Street Station, April 16 1979
An Easter holiday special returning to Glasgow from Ayr had just drawn away from Platform 4 at Paisley's Gilmour Street Station when it was in a head-on collision with the electric train on the 8.40 p.m. Glasgow to Wemyss Bay Service at Wellneuk Junction. The impact was so great that the diesel engine of the Glasgow bound train was lifted onto the roof of the electric train. Seven people were killed, including both drivers, and 63 were injured. The inquiry established that a signal was passed at danger resulting in the collision.

126. Train crash at Paisley, May 20 1958

127, 128. Falkirk rail tragedy, July 30, 1984

The rush hour 5.30 p.m. service from Edinburgh to Glasgow was travelling at about 80 m.p.h. when it hit a bullock which had strayed onto the line half a mile west of Polmont Station. Thirteen people were killed and 44 injured in what was then Britain's worst rail accident for 17 years. The aerial picture shows the leading carriage on its side on the embankment (right). The second carriage, lying at an angle on the left, detached itself and demolished a wall before crashing into the fifth coach. The locomotive is at the rear, controlled remotely by the driver in the front cab. The only fortunate aspect of this sudden disaster was that the driver of an express train from Glasgow, packed with Edinburgh bound commuters, who was running one minute late, spotted the accident as it actually occurred and was able to pull up his train a few hundred yards from the wreckage in time to avert an even worse catastrophe. The stretch of line near Polmont has experienced a series of accidents over the years, including that of February 1962 and, on August 5 1983, three track men were killed near the same spot.

WINES FOR THE
FESTIVE SEASON
BAILEY'S
Quality Wine Merchants
GLASGOW, EDINBURGH, PAISLEY,
GREENOCK, HAMILTON, AYR.
IRVINE, TROON.

SCOTLAND'S NATIONAL NEWSPAPER

Daily Record

Abune them a'
LANG'S
Old
SCOTCH WHISKY

ESTABLISHED 1895.   No. 18,479.   MONDAY, DECEMBER 27, 1954.   A KEMSLEY NEWSPAPER 1½d.

HEAVY RAIN   12 KNOT WIND FROM SOUTH WEST   CLOUD LEVEL 700 FEET

FIRST WRECKAGE HERE — ½ MILE — START OF TARMAC — RUTS & SCARS ON GRASS

TEST PILOTS PROBE THE THREE BIG RIDDLES OF AIR TRAGEDY

DID THE B.O.A.C. STRATOCRUISER WHICH CRASHED AT PRESTWICK ON CHRISTMAS MORNING WITH THE LOSS OF 28 LIVES STRIKE SOFT EARTH BEFORE HITTING THE RUNWAY?

Did it hit a flight of seagulls before turning over and exploding into flames? Or did a sudden gust of wind on the pitiless rainy morning with a low cloud ceiling cause the plane to sway violently and touch the grass verge before the runway?

B.O.A.C. and Ministry of Civil Aviation experts, grim-faced and weary, spent all day yesterday at Prestwick Airport puzzling these theories and trying to discover what caused the plane to topple and overturn as it was coming in to land.

They called for weather reports, for ceiling height, for everything that might have a bearing on the disaster. And still the questions were asked. Was the ill-fated 80-ton plane Cathay talked down by ground control approach (G.C.A.) as had been reported?

There was no confirmation, but on instructions from the Ministry test flights were carried out to check on G.C.A. and the landing aids and equipment in use at the time of the accident. The investigators did not fly in the aircraft, but later received the pilot's report.

Using G.C.A., the pilot is guided by radar to his line-up over the runway, but from 400 feet he is on his own.

G.C.A. was regarded as a vital factor, along with the possibility that rut marks on the grass verge 20 yards before the runway could have been caused by the Stratocruiser's twin port wheels.

There are three deep indentations.

If they were caused by the plane, why did she hit the ground short of the runway? These were the questions to which answers were sought yesterday as the nation was still stunned and shocked by the magnitude of the tragedy.

Last night Deputy Chief Inspector Duggan explained that one of their difficulties was that some members of the crew, including Capt. Stewart, were not in sufficiently good shape to permit of a lengthy interview.

As weather reports for the airport on Saturday morning came in, it seemed clear that although the conditions were difficult —wet, low cloud ceiling of 700 feet above the runway—they were not unusual.

There was a 12-knot wind, but were the gusts sufficient to topple the giant airliner, sister ship of the Canopus, which took the Queen on her Commonwealth tour? That was another question for the experts.

Eye-witnesses say there was just a slight haze over the airport,

that the plane seemed to be making a normal landing, and the control tower at the airport had received no message from the captain to indicate that anything had gone wrong.

And other puzzling features were studied, too.

(I) After the first ruts, assuming they were made by the Stratocruiser, there is no sign of wreckage for another half a mile.

And beside the ruts the earth has been ploughed up as if cut by the port propeller.

(2) The plane turned over before exploding. Did part of
Continued on Back Page

Continued on Back Page

As investigators spent all day going over the ground studying the Prestwick crash scene, the crew survivors, including the pilot, Edinburgh-born Captain Stewart, stayed at the Marine Hotel, Troon, and remained isolated. Phone-calls remained unanswered. Meals were taken to the captain's room, No. 208. The only people allowed in to see him were the investigators, trying to piece together the last few seconds before the plane exploded. The crew moved about the hotel but were under strict orders to say nothing about the crash.

Captain Stewart
Meals in Room 208

The remains of a seagull picked up on the ground just short of the runway after the crash.

3 BOYS ON A WATER TOWER...

" Record " Reporter

IN a high wind, with heavy rain battering them, three youths lay on the top of a 136-foot-high water tower in Drumchapel, near Glasgow, yesterday, while police and watchmen who had surrounded it, shouted to them to come down.

For almost two hours the three defied the men waiting below them.

When the police realised the youths could not be persuaded to come down, a policeman shouted to them: " If you don't come down now, you'll be there for the rest of the night."

That did the trick. The trio slowly descended the narrow workmen's ladder on the outside of the tower.

The three, who were all wearing sandshoes, were taken to the Marine police office, but were later allowed to go home.

B.O.A.C. chairman Sir Miles Thomas (left) at Prestwick with airport commandant Mr. G. Jeffs.

Nancy Campbell
Her sweetheart saw crash.

Outlook
Mild and dull with rain or drizzle at times; fresh or strong winds.

RADIO, TV—PAGE 5

---

129. KLM crash, Auchenweet Farm, Ayrshire, October 21 1948

On October 21 1948 a KLM Royal Dutch Airlines Constellation aircraft flying from Amsterdam to New York came in to land at Prestwick Airport about half an hour after midnight. Visibility was poor but the aircraft was 'talked down' and was in visual range of the airport when the pilot aborted the landing; as it rose and banked away it fouled an overhead high tension cable. The last radio message from the captain, who was KLM's chief pilot, read: "I have hit something. Going on fire. Attempting to climb." The aircraft crashed at North Auchenweet Farm near Tarbolton and immediately disintegrated (above). Thirty-nine lives were lost; just one Dutch passenger survived. At the time it was Scotland's worst aviation tragedy.

130. BOAC aircraft crashes at Prestwick Airport, December 25 1954

In the early morning of Christmas Day 1954 a BOAC Stratocruiser crashed on landing at Prestwick Airport. It was four hours late leaving London and upon arrival at Prestwick around 3.30 a.m. the cloud base was down to 700 ft. In driving rain it was 'talked down' but the port wheels struck the ground on soft earth some distance short of the runway. The aircraft overturned and caught fire at the edge of the main runway. Twenty-eight passengers and crew died; there were three survivors.

131. Sumburgh Airport disaster, July 31 1979

At four minutes past five on the afternoon of July 31 1979 a Dan Air Hawker Siddeley aircraft bound for Aberdeen and carrying 47 oilfield workers crashed on take off at Sumburgh Airport, Shetland. Eye witnesses saw the plane brake heavily at the end of the runway and it then slewed sideways and ran off the runway into the sea. The aircraft broke in two and seventeen men died.

132. Elizabeth Cowe, Dan Air stewardess and the only woman aboard the plane, who was commended for her courage at the inquiry.

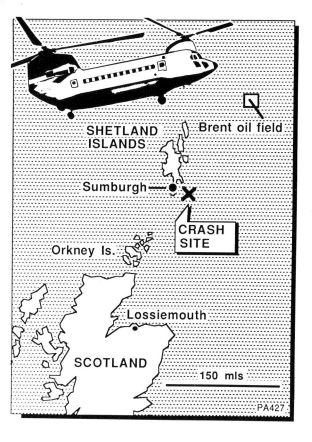

133. Chinook helicopter crash off Shetland, November 6 1986

Forty-five crew and oilrig workers died when a giant Chinook helicpter, on a 135-mile shuttle flight from the Brent oilfield, crashed into the sea off Sumburgh Head, Shetland, a few miles short of its destination: there were just two survivors. The official report on the accident concluded that there was a failure of the aircraft's gear wheel and it was critical of the manufacturers, Boeing of America. Boeing have disputed the conclusion of the official enquiry. The disaster effectively grounded the fleet of three Chinook helicopters operated by British International Helicopters from Aberdeen airport and they did not carry passengers again. Early in 1989 they were sold to Columbia Helicopters of Portland, Oregon.

134. A Chinook helicopter, in the livery of British Airways, but otherwise like the one that crashed.

135. Bringing wreckage ashore at Sumburgh from the downed helicopter.

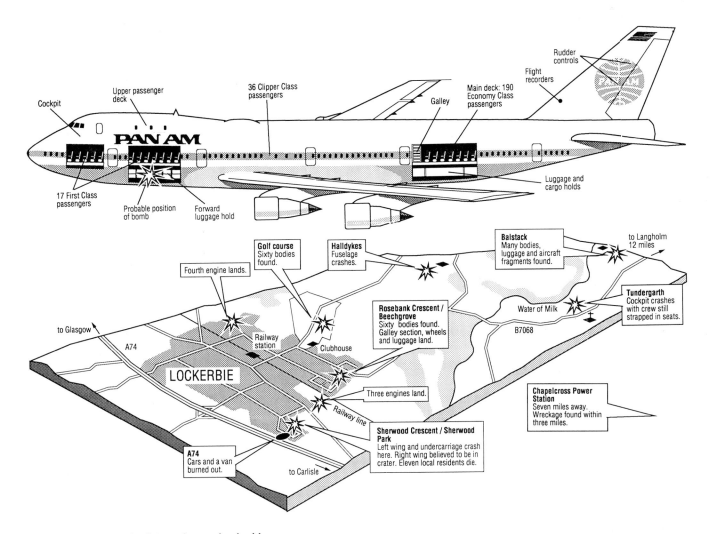

Cockpit

Upper passenger deck

36 Clipper Class passengers

Galley

Main deck: 190 Economy Class passengers

Rudder controls

Flight recorders

PAN AM

17 First Class passengers

Probable position of bomb

Forward luggage hold

Luggage and cargo holds

Golf course
Sixty bodies found.

Fourth engine lands.

Halldykes
Fuselage crashes.

Balstack
Many bodies, luggage and aircraft fragments found.

to Langholm 12 miles

Tundergarth
Cockpit crashes with crew still strapped in seats.

to Glasgow

A74

Railway station

Rosebank Crescent / Beechgrove
Sixty bodies found. Galley section, wheels and luggage land.

Clubhouse

Water of Milk

B7068

LOCKERBIE

Three engines land.

Railway line

Chapelcross Power Station
Seven miles away. Wreckage found within three miles.

A74
Cars and a van burned out.

to Carlisle

Sherwood Crescent / Sherwood Park
Left wing and undercarriage crash here. Right wing believed to be in crater. Eleven local residents die.

136. Pan Am 747 Jumbo Jet crashes on Lockerbie, December 21 1988

At seven o'clock on the evening of Wednesday December 21 1988 Flight PA 103, a Pan Am Boeing 747 Jumbo Jet, registered number N739PA, disappeared from the radar screen at Prestwick air traffic control. The Jumbo, with 259 passengers and crew aboard, was en route from London Heathrow to New York's John F Kennedy airport. Without warning, the aircraft disintegrated at 31,000 feet. Until the flight's transponder return disappeared from controllers' radar screens there was no indication of any problem: the aircraft had been transferred normally from London air traffic control (ATC) to Scottish and then on to Oceanic. Primary radar tapes showed the aircraft breaking into five sections. There was no Mayday call, or transponder selection, and those on the ground were unaware of the catastrophe six miles up for another three minutes, when parts of the stricken 'plane, some now burning fiercely, ploughed into the town of Lockerbie, destroying houses and setting fire to cars and a van on the nearby A74 trunk road.

Wreckage and bodies were scattered over a wide area in six main locations. Most of the wreckage fell to the east of the A74 trunk road and stretched over 6/8 mile east/west path just over a mile wide. A severed wing tore a swathe of destruction through the south side of the town and a massive explosion created a crater 40-foot deep, 50 yards long and 20 yards wide beside the A74. The whole area was littered with burning debris; houses caught fire and four in the direct path of the aircraft simply disappeared in the explosion. The town's Sherwood Crescent was decimated with sixteen houses destroyed or rendered uninhabitable.

The burning tail and rear fuselage plummeted to the earth in the town's council estate of Rosebank catching the end of a terraced row of houses. The cockpit section crashed, remarkably intact, three miles away at Tundergarth Hill, short of

'the other wreckage, the pilot and co-pilot still strapped inside. More than 60 bodies rained onto the local golf course, littering the fairways and bunkers. Other bodies landed in gardens, on rooftops and inside the houses in attics and roofspaces. The tail section landed many miles away near the Borders town of Langholm.

All aboard the plane died and 11 local residents were killed, bringing a death toll of 270. Debris from the aircraft was discovered as far as 80 miles away and bodies of the passengers were scattered over a ten mile radius. At Lockerbie there had occurred the worst disaster in British aviation history and the greatest disaster in Scotland for over a century. The horror of the incident was intensified by the suspicion, which was confirmed a week later, that the sudden catastrophe was the result of sabotage by terrorists. The tragedy of the town of Lockerbie and the ill-fated plane full of unsuspecting passengers flying to America for Christmas took on a new and sinister international aspect as teams of investigators, insurance assessors, experts on terrorism and, even, FBI men and Israeli policemen arrived in the Borders town.

137. The small town of Lockerbie was showered with pieces of aircraft wreckage — all of which were gathered up and painstakingly pieced together by crash investigators. This was a comparatively large piece . . .

138. An aerial view of the massive crater gouged out by the exploding fuselage section of the 747 jet. To the left, is the Sherwood Crescent area of the town which suffered so severely in the explosion and fire which followed.

139. A dramatic view taken at dusk of rescuted plane full of unsuspectinge activities on Tundergarth Hill, where the nosecone section landed.

140. The crater at Sherwood Crescent.

141, 143. Debris littered fields and the busy A74 main trunk road between Glasgow and England.

142. A wing of the aircraft sliced through houses in the town's Rosebank area causing devastation reminiscent of some wartime blitz.

A D M I N I S T R A T I V E N O T I C E

American Embassy, MOSCOW

December 13, 1988

TO   : All Embassy Employees

SUBJECT: Threat to Civil Aviation

Post has been notified by the Federal Aviation Administration
that on December 5, 1988, an unidentified individual telephoned
a U.S. diplomatic facility in Europe and stated that sometime
within the next two weeks there would be a bombing attempt
against a Pan American aircraft flying from Frankfurt to the
United States.

The FAA reports that the reliability of the information cannot
be assessed at this point, but the appropriate police authorities
have been notified and are pursuing the matter. Pan Am has also
been notified.

In view of the lack of confirmation of this information, post
leaves to the discretion of individual travelers any decisions
on altering personal travel plans or changing to another
American carrier. This does not absolve the traveler from
flying an American carrier.

William C. Kelly
Administrative Counselor

(MOSB1) MOSCOW, Dec. 22--BOMB THREAT--A memo distributed to
American diplomats in Moscow by the U.S. Embassy warned of a bomb
threat against a Pan Am plane. A Pan Am plane exploded Wednesday
over Scotland, killing all 258 people aboard. A copy of the memo
was obtained Thursday by The Associated Press. (AP LaserPhoto)
(ark) 1988.

144. Some controversy was excited by the perceived failure of the British and U S governments to make knowledge available to the public of a terrorist threat made to American passenger aircraft a few weeks previously. This notice was posted for the information of staff at the U S Embassy in Moscow. Mr Paul Channon, the Transport Secretary, was advised of the threat but decided not to make it public. At the end of February 1989 he advised that, in his view, it was not relevant to the attack.

145. Prince Andrew made a somewhat controversial visit to Lockerbie the day after the crash. His possibly tactless expression of sympathy for the Americans aboard, rather than locals killed, and observations on the statistical likelihood of an accident of the type, were not widely welcomed in the town.

146. Prince Charles was perceived as salvaging the situation for the Royal Family with a more thoughtful and tactful approach when he appeared in Lockerbie a month after the disaster. He inspects damage in the Serwood Crescent area, on the edge of the crater.

147. Opposite: The last resting place of the nose cone section on Tundergarth Hill.

148. A poignant view at dusk of a damaged house in Sherwood Crescent, the vapour trail of a jet visible in the distance.

149. The painstakingly reconstructed baggage container which held the bag which, in turn, contained the bomb which blew up Flight PA 103. It was displayed to the press on February 16 1989, less than two months after the disaster.

150. From the Prince of Wales, flowers and a note of sympathy.

EXPLOSION & COLLAPSE

151. An 1880 engraving depicts the scene as news of a pit disaster reaches the local community.

Britain's worst mining disaster was at Senghenydd, Glamorgan, in October 1913 when 439 miners died in an explosion and although Scotland has not experienced a single event on this catastrophic scale, pit disasters were once an all too familiar feature of life in many parts of Scotland. The country's worst pit disaster was at Blantyre Colliery on October 22 1877 when 207 miners were killed in a firedamp explosion, assumed to have been caused either by shot-firing or a defective safety lamp. Mauricewood Colliery, Penicuik, was the scene of another accident marked by serious loss of life in September 1889

when 70 miners lost their lives in an underground fire, the cause of which is unknown.

Mining disasters tend to fall into a number of quite specific categories. Most common are explosions, usually associated with firedamp, and which tend to be ignited by naked, open lights or defective safety lamps (the second Blantyre disaster in 1879 when 25 men died; Udston, Lanarkshire, in 1887 when 73 miners died; Cadder, Lanarkshire, 1913, where 22 miners died; and Burngrange, Midlothian, 1947, where 15 miners died after an ignition caused by flame from open acetylene lamps), shot-firing

(Auchinraith, Lanarkshire, in 1930 in which six miners were killed; Cardowan, Lanarkshire, in 1932 in which 11 died), spontaneous combustion, sparking from faulty machinery or electrical equipment (Auchengeich, Lanarkshire, in 1959), or some unestablished cause. Some explosions have been associated with coaldust, which in its own way can be as lethal as firedamp: the explosion at Valleyfield (1939) was spread through the mine by accumulated coaldust.

Extreme negligence seems to have been associated with the firedamp explosion at Gartshore in Dunbartonshire in 1923 which claimed the lives of eight underground workers. Bricklayers were working underground with naked lights on two retaining walls, contrary to the instructions of the manager.

The disaster at Lindsay Colliery in Fife (1957) in which nine miners died highlighted the dangers of cigarettes and matches below ground. Again the enquiry pointed to incomplete supervision at the pit and blamed the disaster on "a match struck for the purpose of smoking". Although not responsible for the disaster, it also emerged that explosives had been introduced into the pit with a lack of supervision. The horror at this accident was intensified by the fact that it came only a month after an accumulation of gas caused an explosion, the effects of which were exacerabated by inadequate ventilation, at Kames Colliery in Ayrshire and which caused the deaths of 17 miners.

Less common were roof falls (Seafield Colliery, 1973) and inundations where water flooded in from old, neighbouring workings. Six miners died at Devon Colliery in Clackmannanshire in March 1897 after an inrush of water from backworkings. At Redding in Stirlingshire, 40 miners were killed in September 1923 after plans failed to indicate that former workings on the higher side of a fault being worked upon were actually connected by a shaft and sump.

Moss or peat in the area of coalfields has produced a hazard largely peculiar to Scotland. When workings are near to the surface and there is an insufficently thick layer of clay to support the moss or peat then a deadly mixture of water and liquefied moss can pour into the mine as a hole appears on the surface — as happened at Donibristle (1901) and Stanrigg & Arbuckle Colliery (1918). Although 58 workers managed to escape the latter disaster, 19 men and boys died, and there was a thorough investigation The court of enquiry concluded that steps ought to be taken to ascertain the depth and the thickness of the strata between coal workings and moss should be at least 60 feet above, or ten times the thickness of the seam, whichever was the greater. This recommendation was embodied in the Moss Regulation of 1920, or Moss Regulation 29 as it became known, but it is doubtful as to how rigorously it was enforced. In 1950, a remarkably similar set of circumstances involving an inrush of moss caused the disaster at Knockshinnoch Colliery.

This gloomy catalogue indicates just how lamentably frequent were serious accidents at mines in Scotland. There were scenes of distressing sameness when news of mishap below ground became known. Wives and mothers, relatives and friends would flock to the pithead to wait anxiously for news. The rescue squads would arrive and work underground in relays. There would be anxious enquiries as they returned to the surface but all too often there would simply be the shake of a head to signify progress. If efforts were successful then the pithead siren would hoot out the good news. In the only book ever published on British pit disasters, Helen and Baron Duckham identify the essence and effect of disaster on a traditional coalmining area: "A colliery disaster strikes and withers a whole community. The toll of a shipwreck or the carnage of a rail or air disaster is more promiscuous, picking on men and women from many areas and many walks of life . . .".

Gas escape has been a common factor in a number of incidents of explosion, notably at Clarkston in 1971 and the Royal Darroch Hotel in 1983.

One of the most horrific of disasters this century must have been the Ibrox disaster of 1971 when, suddenly and unexpectedly, the New Year Old Firm match turned into tragedy as 66 fans died in a terrible crush of bodies. What is often not realised, though, is that this was actually the last — and the worst — in a series of fatal accidents at Ibrox. At a Scotland — England international in 1902 metal girders supporting a section of wooden terracing collapsed and 25 fans fell to their deaths. More than 500 were injured. On September 16 1961, the very same stairway Number 13, was the scene of an accident in which two were killed and 60 injured when the central wooden barrier collapsed. There were further accidents in 1967 and on January 2 1969 there was a clear warning of the disaster to come when the central — now steel — barrier on Stairway 13 again collapsed.

152. Mauricewood Pit Disaster, September 5 1889
The disaster at Mauricewood was Scotland's worst pit disaster in the last hundred years: 63 miners lost their lives in an underground fire, the cause of which is unknown. Most of the miners died of suffocation, caused when smoke flowed into a ventilation system providing air.

THE DONIBRISTLE COLLIERY

THE WORK OF RESCUE
GOING DOWN TO
THE ENTOMBED MINERS

GATHERING HEATHER AT MOSSMORRAN
AS A MEMENTO

153. Donibristle Colliery, August 26 1901

The disaster which engulfed the No. 12 pit of the Donibristle Colliery Company was particularly horrible. The accident took place within thirty feet of the surface and because of the shallowness of the mine at that point an air shaft was being formed from the workings upwards. Suddenly the ground above gave way and many tons of sand, moss and water poured into the workings. The collapse affected about two acres of the bogland known as Mossmorran. Although five miners were rescued the following day, there was then what *The Scotsman* reporter described as a "melancholy incident": due to the weight of the enormous crowd around the operations, a second collapse occurred as another miner was about to be pulled out. The rescue workings were destroyed and despite efforts to rebuld them, there was another collapse the following day and more of the peat sludge and moss poured into the widening hole. *The Scotsman* reported: "The Nemesis of failure seems to dog with grim pertinacity every step that hosts of willing workers on the Morran Moss put forth . . ." In all eight miners died.

154. Pit disaster at Redding, Stirlingshire, September 25 1923
This memorial parchment was framed and hung above the mantlepiece in many homes in the mining community of Redding, near Polmont. It lists those who died — 40 in all — and the five who survived ten days underground before being hauled to safety. As one survivor put it, "Hell burst through", when water broke through from old workings and onto the 66-man nightshift at Redding No. 23 pit.

155. Mine shaft accident at Fishcross, Clackmannan, May 28 1953

156. Knockshinnoch Castle Colliery, Ayrshire, September 7 1950
In an accident reminiscent of the Donibristle disaster of 1901 (q.v.), 130 miners were trapped 720 feet underground at Knockshinnoch Castle Colliery, near New Cumnock, Ayrshire, after an area of moss about 150 yards by 300 yards became liquified by heavy rain and collapsed into the workings. After a massive rescue operation, the men were reached through old workings at Bank Colliery more than a mile away while miners, farmers and other workers on the surface poured bales of hay and straw, tree trunks and pit props into the crater, almost the size of a football pitch, which had opened up in an attempt to stem the flow into the mine of peaty mud. A total of 118 miners were saved; twelve died as did one rescue worker.

Scenes from the Fife pit disaster. Left—Men at the pithead anxiously question a rescue worker. Above—Bringing up one of the bodies. Right—A picture that tells the whole story of the women's grim wait for news of their menfolk.

158. Accident at Whitrigg Colliery, East Whitburn, May 10 1962

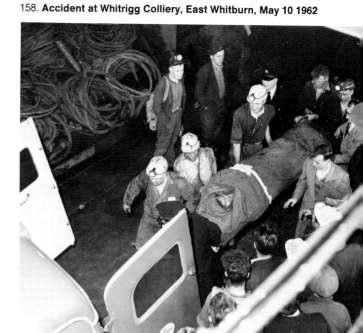

Village Of Mourning For 35 Pit Victims

BY "SUNDAY MAIL" STAFF REPORTERS

THE most tragic village in Scotland to-day is the mining community of Valleyfield, on the north shore of the River Forth near Rosyth. By the disastrous explosion yesterday morning in Valleyfield Colliery, which resulted in the death of 35 men and serious injuries to two others, no fewer than 25 heads of families in the village, which comprises 500 households, have lost their lives.

While the rescue work was proceeding the sound of anti-aircraft guns to the north could be heard by those who were keeping a lonely vigil at the pithead.

A poignant feature of the disaster is the fact that most of the victims are young men and only five of them are unmarried.

Majority of those who lost their lives leave not only sorrowing wives but large families.

The disaster occurred about 3.45 in the morning when an explosion of firedamp annihilated those working the Diamond section of the pit which is about a mile from the pit bottom.

The pit is situated virtually at the water's edge and the workings extend beneath the River Forth. The blast spread through the workings from the Diamond section to the Culross section adjoining.

So devastating was the force of the concussion that not a single man in the Diamond section escaped alive. Most of the men succumbed to burning injuries and the remainder of the casualties were caused by concussion.

TRAGIC PROCESSION

Thomas Kerr, who died after admission to the Dunfermline Infirmary, managed to struggle despite his terrible injuries, to the telephone underground. Weakly he managed to 'phone to the surface and tell them of the disaster which had overtaken them.

Kerr was one of the first to be rescued. He was taken to the infirmary and before he lapsed into unconsciousness learned that his son, Thomas Kerr, jun., who was employed as a fireman in the pit, was among those who had been fatally injured.

KING'S MESSAGE

In connection with the disaster the King sent the following telegram to the Earl of Elgin and Kincardine, Lord Lieutenant of Fifeshire:—

"The Queen and I are deeply grieved to hear of the disaster at Valleyfield Colliery. Will you please convey our heartfelt sympathy to those who have been so sadly bereaved and keep us informed of the condition of the injured and of the progress of the rescue work."

The following message was sent from the Prime Minister to the Fife Coal Company:—

"I have just heard this morning of the heavy loss of life in the explosion at Valleyfield Colliery and I wish to express my profound sympathy with all those so suddenly and tragically bereaved."

Doctor's Ordeal

Begrimed, and with a crash helmet on his head, Dr. Reid told a graphic story.

"There was no apparatus available to protect the rescue party from the white damp which followed the explosion, but in spite of this handicap they persisted in their heroic endeavour to rescue any who might still survive.

Within a matter of minutes news of the disaster spread through the village of Valleyfield, and in the moonlight a tragic procession of mothers and wives with coats thrown hastily over their night garments flocked down the roadway to the pithead.

The first rescue party was led by Mr. Robert Aitchison, manager of the colliery, and Mr. C. C. Reid, general manager of the Fife Coal Co., who own the pit. Included in this party also was Dr. William Reid, son of Mr. Reid.

EXPLOSION HAVOC

was held up until the rescue brigade from Cowdenbeath arrived on the scene with the respirators and oxygen apparatus. I remained below until I was satisfied that there was not the slightest hope of any of those remaining in the pit being still alive"

Dr. Reid showed signs of exhaustion, but despite his ordeal he remained at the pithead so that he might be able to render aid.

WOMEN COLLAPSE

In the cold light of the morning, the tragic congregation of wives, mothers and villagers at the pithead was swelled by people from the district.

Long before the bodies of the victims were recovered the manager was able to issue a complete list of the dead.

Late last night 15 bodies had been brought to the surface. The blacksmith's shop adjoining the shed was transformed into a temporary mortuary. Mothers and wives left the mortuary in a state of collapse, borne up by their friends.

Joseph White was among those who formally identified the dead. Twelve hours previously he had been working with the men at the coal face. He considers himself as the luckiest man alive. With John Philip, also of Valleyfield, he was working in the affected section until about 11 o'clock on Friday night. He was then instructed to proceed to another section.

Robert Lang, engineer, and John M'Intyre, electrician, were of the Diamond section until for about two minutes before the disaster occurred. Their names figure in the death roll.

"The ears of the killed range from 22 to 61. William Devlin was married only last July. He was a well-known football player and appeared regularly for a local junior club.

Harry Toal was married about a year ago. He leaves a widow and a young child.

Seven-year-old twin sons are mourning the death of James Spowart, a widower. Bert Keegan was also a widower and is survived by one son who also works in the pit.

Another victim, David Cairns, is well-known as secretary of the Valleyfield football club.

Mrs. Toal of Valleyfield village had two sons and a son-in-law working in the pit at the time of the disaster. Her son, Harry, was killed and her second son, George Toal, junr., of Woodhead Street, High Valleyfield, is now in hospital. Her son-in-law was working in another section, and escaped unscathed.

SAVES BOY EVACUEE

THE heroism of an Argyll police constable saved the life of a boy evacuee from Glasgow who fell into the sea at Loch Etive.

Police Constable John Macarthur, Taynuilt, was returning from Glen Etive in a small motorboat, the other passengers being Mrs. O'Callaghan, 18 Nethan Street, Govan, and her six children, who were returning home.

Nearing Taynuilt Pier, one of the children, Eugene, aged eight, fell overboard.

Constable Macarthur jumped into the sea fully clothed and succeeded in bringing the boy ashore.

Pumpman's Heroism

A heroic part in the disaster was played by David Anderson, 22 Valleyfield Avenue, a pumpman in the Culross section.

His prompt action in raising the alarm in the face of grave danger undoubtedly minimised the death-roll.

Anderson was walking at the pit bottom when the force of the concussion knocked him to the ground. The pressure of fumes was speedily evident and as he tried to make his escape he was conscious of a growing weakness about the legs.

"When the explosion occurred," said Anderson, "I tried to make my way back to Pump No. 1.

"Near No. 1 pump I saw the bodies of men lying all around, but I was only able to drag myself to the pump where a revolving fan was creating a current of fresh air. I shouted to the men: 'Come in here, there is some fresh air.' I was too weak myself to assist them but seven or eight of my comrades were able to crowd round the fan. We remained there until the rescue party arrived and assisted us to the pithead."

NAMES OF DEAD

The following are the names of the victims of the disaster:—

DEAD

COLIN MORRISON, 18 Woodhead Street, High Valleyfield.
ROBERT M'FARLANE, Main Street, Newmills.
ARCHIBALD ANDERSON, 44 Abbey Crescent, High Valleyfield.
THOMAS CAMPBELL, Main Street, Newmills.
THOMAS CLARK, 54 Abbey Crescent, High Valleyfield.
ALEXANDER PATERSON, 19 Abbey Crescent, High Valleyfield.
DAVID HOGG, Hawthorn Cottages, Carnock.
JAMES IRVINE, West End, Low Valleyfield.
WM. DEVLIN, 12 Woodhead Street, High Valleyfield.
ROBERT NICHOLSON, North Road, Saline.
ARTHUR DOOHAN, Burns Street, High Valleyfield.
DUNCAN EWING, 22 Dundonald Terrace, Low Valleyfield.
PETER MARTIN, 5 Abbey Crescent, High Valleyfield.
DAVID BAILIE, The Ness, Torryburn.
MICHAEL MURRAY, Burns Street, High Valleyfield.
AUBREY GAULD, Mid Row, Hill of Beath.
EDWARD LINK, Braeside Cottage, Low Valleyfield.
JAMES M'FADZEAN, Preston Crescent, High Valleyfield.

ALEXANDER LAWRIE, Balbridgeburn, Dunfermline.
MICHAEL TINNEY, Woodhead Street, High Valleyfield.
EDWARD GLASS, 16 Dundonald Terrace, Low Valleyfield.
DAVID CAIRNS, Preston Street, High Valleyfield.
ROBERT WRIGHT, Dunimarle, High Valleyfield.
PETER GILLIARD, Abbey Crescent, High Valleyfield.
JOHN BROWN, Beaumont Street, Low Valleyfield.
ROBERT LANG, Preston Crescent, High Valleyfield.
ALEXANDER CHRISTIE, St. Mungo, Culross.
JOHN M'INTYRE, Preston Crescent, High Valleyfield.
THOMAS KERR, jun., Abbey Crescent, High Valleyfield.
HENRY TOLL, Preston Crescent, High Valleyfield.
JAMES SPOWART, jun., Tinsilan Crescent, Newmills.
BERT KEEGAN, Woodhead Street, High Valleyfield.
WILLIAM RAMAGE, Blairwood Terrace, Oakley.
ALEXANDER BANKS, East Avenue, Blairhall (died in hospital).
THOMAS KERR, senior, Abbey Crescent, High Valleyfield (died in hospital).

INJURED

John Morgan, Culross.
George Toll, jun., Woodhead Street, High Valleyfield.

157. Explosion at Valleyfield Colliery, Fife, October 28 1939

The explosion at Valleyfield, near Rosyth in Fife, was thought to have been caused in the first instance by shot-firing but its extraordinary violence and spread throughout the mine was attributed to coaldust accumulated in the mine. The explosion occurred at 3.45 a.m. in the Diamond section of the pit, the workings of which extended beneath the River Forth. As the *Sunday Mail* reported: "Within a matter of minutes news of the disaster spread through the village of Valleyfield, and in the moonlight a tragic procession of mothers and wives with coats thrown hastily over their night garments flocked down the roadway to the pit". Rescuers went down the white damp affected mine following the explosion with canaries in cages, but the birds quickly succumbed and efforts were abandoned until the rescue brigade from Cowdenbeath arrived. The enquiry pinpointed coaldust, absence of stonedusting and lack of proper supervision: 35 miners died.

159. Anxious crowds gather at the pithead, Auchengeich Colliery.

160, 161. Auchengeich Colliery, Chryston, Lanarkshire, September 18 1959

The fire at Auchengeich Colliery started with an electrical fault in a fan 1.000 feet below ground and developed into what was Scotland's worst pit disaster of the century. A train of bogies taking workers to the coal face to start the day's work ran into smoke 300 yards from the pit bottom and was brought to a halt. Of the squad of 48 men, only one managed to make his way through the smoke to safety. Firefighters and rescue workers were unable to save the 47 trapped men and that same evening the decision was taken to flood the burning pit. Thus came to an end mining, which had been started at Auchengeich in 1905 and which had continued, the only interruption being an accident in 1931 which claimed five lives.

162. Rescue workers go underground at Auchengeich.

163. Cardowan Colliery, Lanarkshire, July 25 1960

Three men were killed and seven members of a Coatbridge mine rescue team injured in an underground explosion at Cardowan Colliery, Stepps. At 7 p.m. there was an ignition of firedamp whilst work was going on to make the mine safe for the return to work after the summer holiday: the previous January there had been a serious fire at the colliery and work was being undertaken to reopen the affected sections. This photograph shows members of the Coatbridge mine rescue team underground.

164. Mobile mine rescue headquarters vehicle at Coatbridge, Lanarkshire.

165. Michael Colliery disaster, Fife, September 9 1967 (above)

Spontaneous combustion underground caused a serious fire at Michael Colliery, East Wemyss, Fife, which claimed the lives of nine miners. The fire was followed by flooding after the main electrical cable to the pumps burned through and much of the underground workings were destroyed. In this aerial view, fire can be seen pouring from the pit. As a result of the incident, the colliery could not be saved and had to be closed.

166. Accident at Seafield Colliery, Fife, May 10 1973

Five miners died after a roof fall at Seafield Colliery in Fife. Here rescue workers return from underground.

167. The area of the roof fall at Seafield Colliery.

168. Aberdeen zoology building collapse, November 1 1966
The framework of Aberdeen University's new zoology building was almost complete and workmen had virtually no warning of its collapse on a blustery November afternoon. The building collapsed just like the proverbial deck of cards and five men died beneath the reinforced steel and concrete. It was later established that it had insufficient longitudinal rigidy under construction: inset is a photograph of the building taken shortly before it collapsed.

169. Stairway collapse at Ibrox football ground, January 2 1971

There were more than 80,000 spectators gathered for the traditional New Year local derby match between Rangers and Celtic at Ibrox football ground. As fans exited from the ground down Stairway 13 Celtic scored in the 89th minute and, 75 seconds later in injury time, Rangers equalised with a free kick opportunity. There was pandemonium on the terraces and at the exits some tried to turn back and others pushed on. On Stairway 13 the exiting crowd was densely packed and had its own momentum independent of the individuals making it up. One fan who was being carried on another's shoulders was seen to topple forward into the crowd and others were pushed forward. The downward pressure caused those falling to collapse on top of those already on the ground and within a few minutes bodies were piled six feet deep on the stair and barriers and handrails were bent and twisted. A massive emergency operation was immediately launched but 66 fans died from suffocation or traumatic asphyxia. The fatal accident inquiry which was set up subsequently asked for controls on the number of people using Stairway 13 and, generally, on "methods of egress from football grounds". There was no finding against Rangers although, in subsequent litigation, a Sheriff criticised the Club for not taking adequate precautions following previous accidents. In the end of the day, Rangers' insurers paid out more than £ 500,000 in compensation. The Ibrox disaster enjoyed the dubious distinction of Britain's worst sporting disaster until April 15 1989 when 95 Liverpool fans died in the crush at Sheffield's Hillsborough ground during the first few minutes of the FA Cup semi-final betwen Liverpool and Notts Forest.

170. Bodies are laid out at Ibrox.

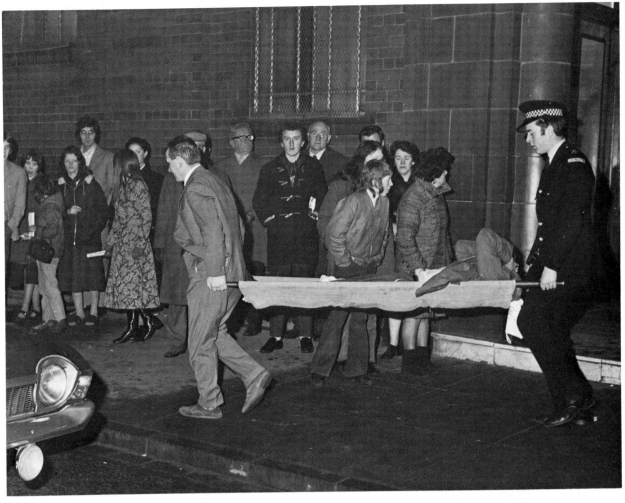

171. Celtic coach Neilly Mochan and a police cadet carry an injured fan to one of the waiting ambulances.

172. Following the collapse on the stairway 13, ambulances queue outside Ibrox stadium.

173. **Clarkston gas explosion, October 21 1971**

Just after 3 p.m. hundreds of people were shopping in the Clarkston shopping centre on the outskirts of Glasgow. A huge explosion tore apart the centre of a block of 26 shops and the structure collapsed like a pack of cards. Most of the casualties were women shoppers or shop assistants: 20 people were killed and 105 injured as a shoe shop, a fruiterer's, a gown shop, a radio rental shop, a newsagent's and a bakery were all devastated. The blast also destroyed a double decker bus outside the block of shops. Following a gas leak, three Gas Board workmen were digging up the gas main running outside the shops. The rescue operations were difficult and extended by reason of the construction of the shops; steel reinforcement beams had to be cut with burning equipment before heavy lifting cranes could be brought in and all the time there was the fear that there could be further explosions from trapped pockets of gas. Clarkston was the worst disaster in Renfrewshire since the Second World War.

174, 175. **Royal Darroch Hotel explosion, October 25 1983**

Two minutes after reporting a smell of gas, six guests and hotel workers died and 15 others were injured when the Royal Darroch Hotel at Cults, Aberdeen, was wrecked by a gas blast at 8.45 a.m. The enormous explosion was heard miles away, debris was thrown a quarter of a mile and a pall of smoke and dust spread for over a mile. The 11-year-old three storey building was reduced to rubble and hotel owner Reo Stakis said, "If I had not seen it with my own eyes I would not have believed an explosion could cause such damage."

176, 177, 178. John Cobb dies on Loch Ness, September 29 1952

John Cobb was the fastest man on land in 1952 when he made his attempt on the world water speed record on Loch Ness. He arrived with his 31-foot Railton-Vosperjet speedboat *Crusader* (*below left*) in Drumnadrochit at the end of August and after practice and modifications he made his official attempt on September 29. As the 6,000 h.p. speedboat streaked across the water (*below right*), a white foam wake corled up astern. Then came a series of bumps and *Crusader* broke into four pieces. Cobb died instantaneously. But just seconds before he was killed he had covered the measured mile in 17.4 seconds — an average speed of 206.89 m.p.h. — which mede him, briefly, the fastest man on water. The accident is believed to have been caused by the craft hitting the bow waves of attendant speedboats.

ENEMY ACTION & WAR

179. An artist's impression of the sinking of H M S *Hampshire*.

The scale and frequency of wartime disasters inevitably put them into a different category. They are also, of course, essentially deliberate in nature and are not, therefore, considered in the same context as the vast majority of peacetime sinkings, fires and explosions. There are a number of books available, or in preparation, on Scotland's wartime experience and the reader is referred to these for a fuller survey. Just a few major incidents are covered here.

There were persistent and consistently damaging air attacks on Aberdeen and the north east of Scotland throughout the early years of the war and then, in 1943, the most serious, massed bomber raid. Aberdeen, it is rarely recognised, suffered grievously from the attentions

of German bombers, despite the fact that Clydebank has tended to become synonymous with the Scottish experience. The two nights of the blitz of March 1941 were indeed terrible in terms of the concentrated nature of the attack but, fortunately, they were not to be repeated. During those same two nights Glasgow actually fared somewhat worse in terms of loss of life but the damage was more widespread throughout the city. In two nights of bombing more than 1200 lives were lost — 528 in Clydebank. Greenock, Gourock and Dumbarton were the targets of similar massed attacks May 5—7 1941 but these were to be the last great air offensives against the Clyde. Greenock came off worst — 280 died — while Dumbarton's decoy strategy served the town well: decoy fires were set off in a dummy town made of wood and canvas high on the hill above Dumbarton.

The resources devoted by the German Navy to winning the Battle of the Atlantic drew the Clyde into the very forefront of the war at sea. Great convoys — and great ships like the *Queen Elizabeth* and *Queen Mary* — gathered at the Tail o' the Bank. There was a constant traffic of vessels with evacuees and goods — even gold — heading west, and with troops and vital food and fuel supplies arriving from America. A sadder sight was the all too regular appearance of weary survivors from Atlantic sinkings; from ships like the liner *Athenia*, sunk in the first few hours of the war; the liner *Empress of Britain* sunk by dive bombers and torpedo off the coast of Ireland; the evacuee ships *City of Simla*, *Volendam* and *City of Benares* with their bewildered cargoes of refugee children, and even from ships carrying German and Italian internees like the *Arandora Star*.

A number of ships of the Royal Navy were lost off the Scottish coast with terrible loss of life, the single most dramatic disaster being the loss of HMS *Curacao* in 1942 — run down by the troopship *Queen Mary*. This tragic collision was kept secret and only revealed at the end of the war. Twenty miles off the coast in the Western Approaches, on October 2 1942, the cruiser HMS *Curacao*, escorting the 81,000 ton troopship *Queen Mary*, was run down by her charge in the Western Approaches and and 331 officers and crew from her complement of 432 men perished. The *Curacao*, steaming straight ahead, was sliced in two by the bows of the great 1,020-foot long liner, following a zigzag course, which did not reduce speed but steamed on to the Clyde out of reach of possible attackers. On board were 10,000 American soldiers and their lives

could not be risked. However, this effectively condemned many of the crew of *Curacao* to death as the nearest rescue ships, the destroyers *Bramham* and *Cowdray*, were two hours away. All those who witnessed the disaster were sworn to secrecy and it was June 1945 before the relatives of those who died were told. In 1945, the Admiralty brought charges against the Cunard Line over the incident but on January 21 1947 the court established that the *Curacao* was at fault, finding that the normal law of the sea relating to overtaking ships did not apply in the special conditions of wartime convoys.

From the point of view of morale during the Second War, it was dealt a most severe blow in October 1939, at the very beginning of the conflict, when the news came of the sinking of the battleship *Royal Oak* at her anchorage within the very confines of the headquarters of the Fleet at Scapa Flow.

In the First War, HMS *Hawke* was sunk off the east coast by submarine action and more than 400 of her crew lost. The 10,850 ton armoured cruiser HMS *Hampshire* was not only sunk with all of her complement bar 12, but also Admiral Lord Kitchener who was lost on a mission to Russia. Departure from Scapa Flow, Orkney, was delayed by bad weather but it was decided that she should proceed, without escort. At 7.40 on the evening of June 5 she struck a mine off Marwick Head. Out of the 655 men aboard only 12 reached the Orkney coast in safety.

The losses of HMS *Vanguard* in Scapa Flow and HMS *Natal* in the Cromarty Firth have neither been adequately explained but both were probably casualties in the string of ships destroyed by internal explosion, caused by unstable stocks of ammunition carried aboard.

180. **Loss of** *Iolaire*, **January 1 1919**

The loss of the naval yacht *Iolaire* after the end of the First World War was Britain's worst peacetime naval disaster this century. Formerly the luxury sailing yacht *Amalthea*, she was leased to the Admiralty in 1915 and employed as a submarine hunter. Early on New Year's Day 1919 she was approaching Stornoway Harbour on the Island of Lewis on passage from the railhead at Kyle of Lochalsh with 260 returning Lewismen and crew of 24 aboard, mostly ex-Navy men returning from the War (a conflict which had already claimed the lives of more than 1,000 of their fellow islanders). At ten minutes to two she struck a submerged reef, known locally as the Beast of Holm, at the entrance to the harbour and the vessel foundered. Of those aboard, 205 died, all within twenty yards of the shore. The naval inquiry was inconclusive but it was clear to most people that the ship was overloaded (she should in fact have only been carrying 80 persons) and that she was off course, far too near to land, when she struck the rocks — probably having lost sight of Arnish Light at the harbour entrance and, upon regaining sight of the light, an ill-considered change of course resulted in the disaster.

181. This photograph, taken the morning after the stranding of the *Iolaire* shows just how close to land - and safety - she struck.

182. Auxiliary cruiser *Oceanic*, Sept 8 1914, grounds off Foula

At the beginning of the First World Ware the 17,274 ton luxury liner *Oceanic*, operated by the White Star line of Liverpool and sister ship to the ill-fated *Titanic*, was requisitioned by the Admiralty and brought into use as an auxiliary cruiser. When she was launched in 1899 she was then the largest ship in the world. A colourful history ensued: she ran down the British coaster *Kincora* in September 1901 with the loss of seven of the latter vessel's crew and in 1905 there was a mutiny on board which resulted in the conviction of 33 of her crew. In September 1915, operating with the 10th Cruiser Squadron, she grounded on rocks east of the island of Foula, Shetland, as a result of a navigation error combined with a certain amount of confusion on board as a result of her having two captains, her peacetime and naval appointees. Although the Aberdeen trawler *Glenogil* successfully took off 400 ratings and officers, the ship became a total loss. She proved impossible to refloat and in less than a month this very large ship — almost 700 feet long — had disappeared completely. She is the largest ship ever to be wrecked in the Shetland Islands.

183. Loss of HMS *Vanguard*, Scapa Flow, July 9 1917

The 19,250 ton battleship HMS *Vanguard* was destroyed not by enemy action but by a massive internal explosion, probably caused by the deterioration of stocks of high explosive carried aboard. She was blown apart at her anchorage in Scapa Flow and there were only two survivors out of a complement of 806 men. A St Vincent class Dreadnought, she was delivered to the Royal Navy in 1910 and saw action at the Battle of Jutland. The wreck was later raised and scrapped on Tyneside in 1927.

184. "The Battle of May Island", Firth of Forth, January 31 1918

If this incident had not had such tragic consequences, it might have qualified for an episode of *The Navy Lark*. During the course of a night exercise off the Island of May in the Firth of Forth, two K-class submarines were sunk and two further submarines and a cruiser seriously damaged, resulting in the loss of 103 officers and ratings. The controversial K-class submarines — twice as long at 300 feet as any other submarines in existence — had appeared to be jinxed from their introduction, without trials, in the First War. *K-4*, with the future King George VI aboard, dived into the mud and lodged there while *K-13*, built by Fairfords on the Clyde, sank to the bottom of the Gareloch in January 1917 with 80 dockyard workers and crew aboard: only 47 were saved.

In the Forth disaster two separate forces left Rosyth on exercise. The first comprised the cruiser *Ithuriel* leading *K-11*, *K-17*, *K-14*, *K-12* and *K-22* in line-astern, followed by the cruisers *Australia*, *New Zealand*, *Indomitable* and *Inflexible*. The cruiser *Fearless* led the next flotilla of *K-3*, *K-4*, *K-6* and *K-7*, followed by battleships and destroyers. As they headed out to sea, a group fo minesweepers, apparently unaware of the exercise crossed the bows of the first wave as it passed May Island. Chaos followed. *K-14*, shown here, swung around and her steering locked; *K-22* (previously the ill-fated *K-13* now renamed) sliced off her bows. The cruisers bore down on them and *Inflexible* crashed into *K-22*. *Ithuriel* and her submarines turned back to assist but *Fearless* then ploughed into *K-17*. In the confusion *K-6* rammed *K-4*, which sank with no survivors. At that time the crew from *K-17* were in the water but the heavy destroyers and battleships, supposedly arriving to the rescue, steamed into the area and drowned or killed with their screws the survivors in the sea. Only seven from *K-17* survived. Thus ended a particularly inglorious episode in British naval history.

185, 186, 187. Sinking of the German High Seas Fleet, June 21 1919

Of course, whether or not this is considered a disaster depends somewhat one one's standpoint! Some might maintain that the sinking of the entire German High Seas Fleet was quite the opposite: certainly for the salvors it produced a financial opportunity without equal. The scale of the event was staggering: as Dan van der Vat observes in his book *The Grand Scuttle* it was "the gratest single loss of shipping since Man first sat astride a log and floated away from land". More than 400,000 tons of naval shipping were sunk — 52 ships out of a total of 74 anchored in Scapa Flow — on the instructions of Rear-Admiral Ludwig von Reuter. The warships, which made up the main strength of the Imperial Navy's High Seas Fleet, had been interned in Scapa since just after the Armistice in November 1918. There were five battlecruisers, eleven battleships, eight cruisers and 50 destroyers. The scuttling was a carefully planned operation. The flagship *Emden* was seen to fly signals to the rest of the fleet on June 20 and late the next morning she hoisted a pre-arranged code signal: *Schiffe sofort versenken*. At 11.45 a British war artist named Gribble noted German sailors from the *Friedrich der Grosse* throwing bags into boats. She was the first capital ship to sink, at 12.16, folowed by *Koenig Albert* at 12.54. By 14.00 hours eleven more ships had sunk and by 1500 a further three. At 15.50 the *Karlsruhe* went, at 16.45 the *Markgraf* and, last of all, the *Hindenburg* at 17.00. The First British Battle Squadron had left that morning on exercise but was recalled by radio. By the time the first destroyers returned around 14.30 the situation had passed the point of no return. Some ships were successfully run ashore but the scuttling had clearly been well planned. The crew of a British drifter attempted to foil the scuttling of the battleship *Markgraf* and a stuggle ensued in which her Captain was killed and her engineer officer seriously wounded. By the end of the afternoon, only the battleship *Baden*, three cruisers and 18 destroyers remained afload. It was initially the view of the Admiralty that the sunken ships were of no value and did not represent a danger to navigation. They were, in due course, to be disabused of both notions. Several trawlers ran onto the wrecks over the ensuing years and as world stocks of scrap metal became depleted in the 1920s it was realised that there was a cosiderable resource below the waters of Scapa flow.

"Derffbinger's" last Stage

Salving the "Konig Albert"

TOWING SALVED GERMAN BATTLESHIP, SCAPA FLOW.

188. HMS *Royal Oak*, October 14 1939

The loss of the 29150 ton elderly battleship *Royal Oak* (*above*) at her anchorage in Scapa Flow at the very beginning of the Second World War was a major blow to morale: 833 officers and men perished as a result of the torpedo attack by Kapitan Leutnant Gunther Prien in command of *U47*. The battleship was hit by just one torpedo on her starboard bow, just below the waterline, at five past one in the morning. Initially, it was thought that there had been an internal explosion (as had caused many accidents to warships in the First War) and Prien escaped through the inadequately protected or patrolled Kirk Sound, through which he had entered. Twelve minutes after the attack there was a series of explosion and at 01.29 she capsized and sank in less than one hundred feet of water, less than 1,000 yards from the shore. Of her complement, 424 officers and men were saved. Prien later stated that the attack was made by way of revenge for the loss of the German High Seas fleet in Scapa Flow at the end of the First World War.

189. Anxious relatives scan the casualty lists for survivors from the *Royal Oak*.

190. Sinking of the *Athenia*, September 3 1939

Within a few hours of the declaration of war, the S S *Athenia* was sunk in the Atlantic 200 miles west of the Hebrides en route from Liverpool to Montreal. The first survivors were brought back to the Clyde port of Greenock within 48 hours by naval ships.

S.S. POLITICIAN.

191. S S *Politician*, wrecked Eriskay, February 4 1941

The wreck of the S S *Politician* has been immortalised by the writer Compton Mackenzie in his humorous novel *Whisky Galore*, also made into an equally hilarious Ealing comedy of the same title. The 8,000 ton cargo ship left Liverpool under the command of Captain Beaconsfield Worthington with a diverse and valuable cargo which included more than a quarter of a million bottles of whisky, more than £3m. in brand new Jamaican currency, fur coats, perfumes, cosmetics and a whole range of other goods then unavailable in wartime Britain. The cargo was bound for New Orleans and Kingston, Jamaica, and the purpose of certain elements of it remains a mystery to this day, the documents relating to it being kept from public scrutiny until 2016

Off Calvey, on the Island of Eriskay in the outer Hebrides, she went hard aground in heavy weather and poor visibility. For the islanders such a cargo was as manna from heaven — only more useful — and they launched themselves upon what has been called "the biggest freeloading booze bender of all time". The authorities ensured that what they regarded as the valuable cargo was salvaged - but initially ignored the whisky as of little value and too difficult to recover. When the salvage vessel *Ranger* left the scene, the two local Customs & Excise officers proved unequal to controlling the thirsty islanders . . . To this day, there are many dozens of anecdotes about the ensuing game of hide and seek indulged in by the islanders and the authorities. Eventually, the wreck was broken up and the number five hold dynamited to bring these night excursions to an end but, as recently as August 1987, bottles were brought to the surface, at the behest of the *Mail on Sunday* newspaper who engaged divers to blow open a hatch cover in the wreckage more than 30 feet below the surface. There were also, at that time, some extraordinary rumours of intrigue involving the Duke and Duchess of Windsor (he was Governor General of the Bahamas at the time), film actor Errol Flynn (a Nazi sympathiser living in Jamaica) and the British Royal family, allegedly preparing a home in exile in case of invasion. Just the stuff of storybooks of course . . . .

192. Duke of Kent dies in plane crash, August 25 1942

The Duke of Kent, the youngest brother of King Georg VI, set off from a seaplane base in Scotland in a Sunderland flying boat on a special mission to Iceland. After flying only 60 miles, the aircraft crashed in a remote and desolate part of the north of Scotland near Braemore in Caithness and all 15 passengers on board, including the Duke of Kent, died. The purpose of the mission to Iceland and the circumstances surrounding the crash were, of course, at the time shrouded in wartime secrecy but, to this day, there is still speculation about the incident and there are some interesting, if colourful, theories linking it to Rudolph Hess and the projected 'World Air Force'. Opposite is a photograph taken in 1940 of the Duke of Kent, in the RAF uniform of an Air Commodore, and his family.

193. Clydebank Raid, March 14/15 1941

At the beginning of March 1941 the town of Clydebank was a 47,000 strong shipbuilding-based community. More than 90% of the children who had been evacuated in 1939 were now back with their families in the town's 12,000 crowded and crumbling tenements. The effects of the two night raids by a total of 439 bombers were devastating: out of the stock of 12,000 houses only seven were undamaged. The nocturnal population dropped from 50,000 to 2,000 overnight and even a year later something like 35,000 people were still without homes, despite the efforts of 800 workers repairing the housing stock.

194. Massed bomber attack on Aberdeen, April 21 1943

Although Aberdeen was the most frequently bombed city in Scotland, most of the raids were impulsive 'tip and run' affairs which did not cause extensive damage and loss of life throughout the City. The raid of April 21 1943 was on a much different scale. In a pre-planned air raid 25 Dornier 217s of the Kampf-Geschwader Group 2 swept in from the north of the City as dusk fell causing extensive damage in the Woodside, Hilton, Cattofield, Kittybrewster and George Street areas. Middlefield School, Causewayend Church, Carden Place Episcopal Church, the Royal Mental Hospital, the nurses' home and the Gordon Barracks were all bombed and set alight. The toll was heavy: 98 people were killed and a similar number seriously injured. This is how the Berlin *Illustrierte Zeitung* reported the attack.

So griffen wir Aberdeen an!

Aus dem Bord-Skizzenbuch
des Ritterkreuzträgers
Hauptmann Bornschein

Zwei Pfeile — zwei Phasen.

Dieser Ausschnitt aus dem Luftbild von Aberdeen zeigt die
beiden Angriffsrichtungen schwerer deutscher Kampfflugzeuge
auf die bedeutende schottische Industrie- und Hafenstadt.

„Feuer frei!"

... ein Flakgeschütz auf einem erhöhten Stand wird
überrumpelt und, bevor es überhaupt zum Schuß kommt,
durch entschlossenes Kanonenfeuer meines Bordschützen
ausgeschaltet. Die grell sprühenden Feuerketten wirken
für alle Flugzeuge als Startschuß . . .

Die erste Phase:

. . . . mit mir kurvt der
ganze Verband auf die
Stadt zu. Die große gerade
Straße dient als Wegweiser.
Die Ziele vor Augen,
braust der Verband in
breiter beweglicher Front
dicht über den Häusern
dahin. Es ist ein Schwingen,
Tauchen und Springen
über Türme und Schorn-
steine hinweg. Man muß
aufpassen, daß man nicht
mit dem Nachbarflugzeug
zusammenstößt. Deutlich
heben sich gegen den Hori-
zont die Industriewerke
und die Klötze der Gaso-
meter ab . . .

Die zweite Phase:

. . . . keine der schweren
Bomben verfehlt ihr Ziel.
Die Bordschützen schießen,
was ihre Waffen herge-
ben. Die Luft sprüht von
den leuchtenden Geschoß-
ketten der Bordwaffen und
. . . .
. . . . nation
auf Tr . . . . .
anlagen . . . .
gut . . . .
. . de . . .
wolk . . .
Himm . . .

CHRONOLOGICAL LIST OF ACCIDENTS & DISASTERS 1879 - 1989
featured in this book

1879 - 1889

1879 July 2	Blantyre Colliery explosion kills 25 miners
1879 December 28	Tay Bridge disaster
1881 October 14	Half of Eyemouth fishing fleet lost
1883 July 3	Capsize of the *Daphne* in the Clyde
1884 November 1	Fire at the Star Theatre, Glasgow
1887 May 28	73 miners die in Udston Colliery explosion

1889 - 1989   The Last 100 Years

1889 September 5	Mauricewood Pit disaster
1895 May 31	Underground fire, Kineddar Colliery, Fife
1898 February 4	Barassie rail disaster, Troon
1900 April 24	*St. Rognovald* aground Brough Head, Stronsay
1900 August	Bubonic plague in Glasgow
1901 August 26	Donibristle Colliery disaster
1903 July 27	Rail crash at St Enoch Station, Glasgow
1904 December 31	*Stromboli & Kathleen* collide off Greenock
1905 June 26	Victoria Mills, Galashiels, destroyed by fire
1905 July 7	Peebles Hydropathic burns down
1905 November 19	Glasgow lodging house fire
1906 July 11	Inchgreen runaway train accident
1906 December 28	Elliott Junction railway disaster, Arbroath
1907 February	Meningitis outbreak in Glasgow & Edinburgh
1907 August 9	Barquentine *Celtic* aground, Sandwick, Orkney
1908 December	Heavy snow in northeast Scotland
1909 August 17	Great fire in centre of Glasgow
1911 May 9	Fire at the Empire Theatre, Edinburgh
1912 November	Widespread gales and floods
1913 August 3	Underground fire at Cadder Pit, Lanarkshire
1914 February 28	Torpedo destroyer *Laverock* aground Skelmorlie
1914 April 14	Fife railway disaster, Burntisland
1914 June 15	Carrbridge railway disaster
1914 September 8	Loss of *Oceanic*, Foula, Shetland
1915 May 22	Britain's worst railway disaster at Gretna
1915 October 15	HMS *Hawke* sunk off N.E. Scotland
1915 December 30	Explosion on HMS *Natal* in Cromarty Firth
1916 January 1	Fire at Mugdrum House, Fife
1916 June 5	HMS *Hampshire* sunk off Birsay Head
1917 July 9	HMS *Vanguard* sinks in Scapa Flow
1918 January 31	103 lost in night exercise, Firth of Forth
1919 January 1	Loss of *Iolaire* off Stornoway
1919 June 21	German High Seas Fleet sinks in Scapa Flow

1919 April 28	Crew members lost from Fraserburgh Lifeboat
1920 October 10	Trawler *Ben Namur* ashore Bay of Skaill, Orkney
1921 October 9	Steamer *Rowan* sinks off Clyde
1923 July 28	Gartshore Colliery disaster, Dunbartonshire
1923 September 25	Pit disaster at Redding, Stirlingshire
1924 September 29	Schooner *Kathleen Annie* aground Orkney
1929 December 25	Swedish ship *Ustetind* aground, Walls, Shetland
1929 December 31	Fire at the Glen Cinema, Paisley
1930 April 10	Mail steamer *St Sunniva* ashore Mousa, Shetland
1930 August 30	Firedamp explosion at Auchinraith Colliery
1931 July 3	Swedish steamer *Borg* ashore Birsay Bay, Orkney
1932 November 16	Firedamp explosion at Cardowan Colliery
1937 December 10	Castlecary railway disaster
1939 October 14	*Royal Oak* sunk, Scapa Flow
1939 October 28	Firedamp explosion, Valleyfield Colliery, Fife
1941 March 14/15	Clydebank raid
1941 May 6/7	Raid on Greenock
1941 February 4	S S *Politician* aground, Eriskay
1942 October 2	H M S *Curacao* sunk by T S *Queen Mary*
1942 August 25	Duke of Kent dies in plane crash
1943 April 21	Massed bomber raid on Aberdeen
1947 January 10	Explosion and fire at Burngrange Colliery
1948 August	Widespread flooding
1948 October 21	KLM crash, Tarbolton, Ayrshire
1949 May 4	Fire destroys Graftons' store, Glasgow
1950 June 8	Express train fire, Beattock Summit
1950 September 7	Knockshinnoch Castle Colliery disaster
1951 November	Maryculter floods, Aberdeen
1953 July 18	Floods in Edinburgh
1952 September 29	John Cobb dies aboard *Crusader*, Loch Ness
1953 January	Great storms
1953 January 31	Ferry *Princess Victoria* sinks in Irish Sea
1953 January 31	*Clan Macquarrie* wrecked, Borve, Lewis
1953 January 31	Loss of trawler *Michael Griffith*, Barra
1953 January 31	Two men lost from Islay Lifeboat in recue bid
1953 January 31	Grimsby trawler *Sheldon* lost off Orkney
1953 February 9	Fraserburgh lifeboat overturns
1953 October 27	Six men lost from Arbroath Lifeboat
1953 October 27	Dundee sand ship *Inchmagee* lost
1954 December 25	BOAC Stratocruiser crashes at Prestwick
1955 November 10	Fire at CW Carr Aitkman, Edinburgh

1955 November 11	Fire at C & A Modes, Princes Street, Edinburgh
1956 August 29	Tyne overflows at Haddington; Tweed at Peebles
1957 January 6	Fishery cruiser *Vaila* sinks off coast of Lewis; 5 crew lost
1957 May 9	Fire at Wm. Mutries's, Bell's Brae, Edinburgh
1957 November 19	Explosion at Kames Colliery, Ayrshire
1957 December 14	Explosion at Lindsay Colliery, Fife
1958 January 16	HMS *Barcombe* aground, Mull
1958 May 13	S S *Cliffville* sinks, Meadowside Quay, Glasgow
1958 May 20	Paisley train crash
1958 August 20	Barrowland Ballroom fire, Glasgow
1958 November 17	Swiss cargo ship *Nyon* aground, St Abbs Head
1959 January 9	Fishery cruiser *Freya* capsizes near Wick; 3 crew lost
1959 January 28	Tram blaze, Old Shettleston Road, Glasgow
1959 September 18	Auchengeich Colliery disaster
1959 December 6	North Sea gales
1959 December 6	Trawler *George Robb* aground, Duncansby Head
1959 December 7	Crew lost from Broughty Ferry lifeboat
1959 December 7	North Carr light vessel adrift
1959 December 7	Coaster *Servus* aground, Dunbeath Castle
1959 December 7	Freighter *Anna* aground, St. Combs
1960 February 25	Trawler *Craigievar* aground St. Abbs Head
1960 March 28	Cheapside whisky bond fire, Glasgow
1960 May 6	Submarine *Narwahl* aground, Campbeltown
1960 July 25	Accident at Cardowan Colliery
1960 October 13	S S *Lochiel* aground West Loch Tarbert
1962 February 5	Train crash at Polmont
1962 May 24	Tug *Forager* sinks in Clyde
1962 May 31	Gaumont fire, Edinburgh
1964 January 3	Trawler *Ben Barvas* aground, Pentland Firth
1964 June/July	Aberdeen typhoid epidemic
1966 August 30	Family of seven die in Shettleston fire
1966 November 1	Zoology building collapse, Aberdeen University
1967 September 9	Michael Colliery disaster, Fife
1968 January 15	Gales in west of Scotland: 20 die
1968 November 18	James Watt Street warehouse fire, Glasgow
1969 March 17	Longhope lifeboat overturns
1969 April	Aberdeen Combworks fire
1970 January 21	Fraserburgh lifeboat overturns
1970 May 6	Trawler *Summerside* aground near Aberdeen
1971 January 2	Ibrox disaster
1971 October 21	Clarkston gas explosion
1971 November 21	Cairngorm tragedy
1973 May 10	Roof fall, Seafield Colliery, Fife
1974 January	Polish trawler *Nurzec* aground near Aberdeen
1975 November 5	Fire at Inverary Castle
1977 July 15	PS *Waverley* aground on the Gantocks
1978 January 7	Firemens' strike: Grosvenor Hotel fire
1978 January 7	Firemens' strike: Linwood house fire
1979 April 16	Train crash at Paisley
1979 July 31	Sumburgh Airport disaster
1982 February 26	Cargo ship *Craigantlet* ashore Portpatrick
1983 August 5	Three track workers killed on main line near Polmont
1983 October 25	Royal Darroch Hotel gas explosion, Aberdeen
1984 July 30	Rail disaster at Polmont
1986 July 1	Aberdeen Grammar School fire
1986 November 6	Chinook helicopter crash off Shetland
1988 July 6	*Piper Alpha* disaster in North Sea
1988 July 7	*Seaboard Intrepid* aground Bressay, Shetland
1988 September 22	*Ocean Odyssey* explosion and fire in North Sea
1988 December 21	Pan Am flight PA 103 crashes on Lockerbie
1989 January 13	Fishing boat *Boy Andrew* sinks off Shetland
1989 February 7	Floods sweep away railway bridge, Inverness

Note: This is a chronological list of all the accidents referred to in this book. Although every incident over the last one hundred years involving major loss of life is dealt with, this is only a selective listing in relation to less serious events. The listing for the purpose of this edition ceases at February 28 1989.

195. **For those in need (1)**: a U S military Douglas SC-540 Rescuemaster on the tarmac at Prestwick, 1950.

SCOTLAND'S WORST DISASTERS

Scotland's 12 worst peacetime disasters in the last 100 years

1988 December 21	Lockerbie Pan Am jumbo crash	270 die
1915 May 22	Gretna rail crash	227 die
1919 January 1	Naval yacht *Iolaire* sinks off Lewis	205 die
1988 July 6	Oil rig *Piper Alpha* explosion & fire	167 die
1953 January 31	Ferry *Princess Victoria* sinks	133 die
1929 December 31	Fire at the Glen Cinema, Paisley	70 die
1971 January 2	Ibrox football stadium disaster	66 die
1889 September 5	Mauricewood Pit Disaster	63 die
1959 September 18	Auchengeich Colliery, Lanarkshire	47 die
1986 November 6	Chinook helicopter crash off Shetland	45 die
1923 September 25	Pit disaster, Redding, Stirlingshire	40 die
1905 November 19	Glasgow lodging house fire	39 die
1948 October 21	KLM aircraft crashes near Tarbolton	39 die

196. **For those in need (2)**: The Salvation Army at the pithead, Auchengeich Colliery disaster, 1959.

POSTSCRIPT

A note on causes

Scotland's worst peacetime disaster was caused by an act of deliberate sabotage. With major disasters it is not always possible to clearly apportion blame but human negligence was an identifiable common factor in the Gretna rail crash, the Glen Cinema, the Ibrox disaster and the Glasgow lodging house fire. In the other incidents the cause is less clear cut. Where those in charge do not survive — as in the ferry *Princess Victoria*, *Iolaire* and KLM crash incidents — investigators are at a disadvantage and in all these cases misjudgement rather than negligence may have played a part. Equally, circumstances often combine to produce a wholly unexpected result as, for example, in the loss of the Stranraer—Larne ferry where quite unusually extreme weather associated with the failure of the stern loading doors, inaccurate rendering of position and non-availability of tugs and rescue vessels all came together to produce tragedy from what might otherwise have proved a manageable incident.

Sir Harold Roberts noted in his conclusions to the official enquiry into the November 1957 explosion at Kames Colliery, Ayrshire: "It was the tragically simple story of a combination of errors and misjudgements, not of great danger individually but together leading to disaster — a story paralleled time and again in mining history ...".

And not *just* mining history, it could be added.

197. **For those in need (3)**: The St. Abbs Lifeboat launches down the slipway, August 1951.

SOURCES OF PICTURES

If there are two attributions, then the first relates to the owner, collection or copyright holder. The second, after the /, gives the name of the photographer or artist, if known.